How To Buy, Sell, and Operate
RV Parks and Campgrounds

Written by **Dave Reynolds**

ISBN 978-0-6151-6904-0

Table of Contents

RV Park Investments...
The Beginning

I have met hundreds of people in person and through RVParkStore. com over the years that claim that they would like to own an RV Park or Campground. However, many of these people really did not have any idea what it meant to actually buy an RV Park or Campground and what it all entailed. Answering a few questions by phone or email was not enough to even graze this subject. I believe that many of them meant well and it was more of a dream than a reality to be. Granted it would have been easier for them to have a book or resource to educate and guide them through the process. Before now, there was not such a detailed resource available to help.

My dream is for this book to hit the New York Times Bestseller's list with hundreds of book signing engagements...but the reality is that this book will help many people looking to buy, operate, and sell an RV Park to do so more profitably and avoid many of the mistakes I have seen and made in my years of experience. In fact, after reading this book you may find that you are definitely not interested in this business at all. And that is fine too. Owning an RV Park or Campground is not for everyone.

After reading this book and finding that you are interested in taking the next step and buying a campground the key is to turn yourself into a "Willing Buyer". A willing buyer will have the following qualifications:

- An understanding of how to buy an RV Park
- An understanding of what it entails to own and operate an RV park

- The financial resources to buy an RV Park that meets your goals

- A sense of urgency... you must be actively searching for an RV Park

- And most of all a DESIRE TO BUY!

In most cases, buying an RV Park depends on you, your capital, and the amount of time you spend learning the business and learning from your mistakes. You should only buy an RV Park if you think you can do better than the previous owner. If you do not believe you can do better, this is a recipe for failure. You should be motivated and a self starter and a genuine doer. As the owner of an RV Park you will often wear many hats and do things that you never even thought of. However, owning an RV Park or Campground can be an exciting, fun, and profitable lifestyle or career!

How I Started in the RV Park Business

Before my senior year in high school, my parents bought a suburban and a pull behind camper and we set off for a several week long vacation from Colorado to Florida and many places between here and there. I had never stayed in an RV Park or Campground before that trip and the whole concept was foreign to me. We stayed in KOA's, mom and pop's, and everything in between. Looking back, the only thing my brothers and I cared about was that the RV Park we stayed in that night had a swimming pool to cool off in. How times have changed since then. In many cases, teenagers look forward to wireless internet and cell phone service these days. This is an important thing to consider. Who are you targeting and are you targeting them in the right ways.

The following year, I went away to college – Western State College in Gunnison, Colorado. My family still had the RV and on one of their trips to Gunnison to visit, they took a tour of Blue Mesa Recreational Resort just outside of Gunnison and lo and behold they purchased a membership in the Resort. For me, this was a place to get away from the dorms once in awhile and get some studying done. I spent quite a bit of time there and often thought about owning a resort such as this.

After graduating from college and buying and selling a few single family homes, my investing focus shifted to looking at commercial properties and more specifically, Mobile Home Parks. After a few months of searching, I saw an ad for a Mobile Home and RV Park in Limon, Colorado. The park had about 45 mobile home spaces and 9 overnight spaces. The park was listed for about $275,000. However, the owner wanted to be cashed out and after telling the banks where I was planning to get my down payment from (cash advancing credit cards), they were not at all impressed. The seller said he had found a different buyer so this deal was all but dead.

A few months later, the same owner called me and said that his other buyer didn't go through with it and if I could come up with $50,000 in 10 days, I could assume the notes and own the park. I was all over it. The next day I met with the seller and his attorney and found out that the reason I had to close so quickly was that he was about 10 days from losing the property to foreclosure and was desperate. He didn't have time to find another buyer and I was his last resort. Looking back, I probably should have negotiated a better deal and at least hired an attorney to review the contract I made in the seller's attorney's office as this was my first commercial property transaction. I was nervous to find out that the Seller was in foreclosure and figured that there must be something wrong with the property that I didn't notice on my 30-minute of drive through the park, and around town.

I wouldn't say that I fell in love with the property but I did have my mind set on buying the park and I would make it work one way or another. I was buying this park with cash advances on my credit cards and when I showed up at the bank the day before closing to cash advance 50k from a variation of about 10 credit cards the President of the Bank couldn't believe I was serious about taking all these cash advances from my credit cards in order to buy a TRAILER Park! Well after about 2 hours at the bank and verifying all the information one by one I had a $50,000 cashiers check in hand and was ready to go.

The next day, I showed up to closing in Hugo, Colorado at the most unorganized title company I have ever seen to this day. The paperwork had just been started, they did not own a computer, the two note-holders that I was assuming their notes were there, the

Seller was there and was half drunk and I could tell there was tremendous animosity between the Seller and the note-holders. (Later on, I found out that the Seller bought the property about 9 months beforehand and had never made a payment and had also not made payments for most of the utilities or repairs that were done in the park for the time he owned it) Imagine a very small town in which all the plumbers and electricians had been stiffed and then trying to get someone to the park to do any work!

As the closing statements were being drawn up I noticed that the notes that I was assuming were not the same amounts that I had been told by the Seller. I was supposedly going to be buying the park for $265,000 with $50,000 down and assume a balance of $215,000. The balance on the notes were about $200,000 instead of $215,000 so I had to come up with another $15,000 real fast as I had not insisted on any provisions stating what the amount to be assumed was. Needless to say, I ended up racking up an additional $15k on credit cards to make the deal happen.

I know what you must be thinking… why didn't I threaten to walk away from the deal if the seller didn't come down in price? I was his last hope, if he didn't take the 50k down that day he would get nothing from it tomorrow. Looking back, I could have saved at least the 15k by hiring an attorney for a few hundred dollars to review the contract.

At about 5 pm, I owned my first park. As I was driving back home to Fort Collins it started to hit me that I was now in charge of about 50 lots and owned around 20 park owned mobile homes. I basically had about 5k left on credit and in the bank to work with and needed to come up with a plan. I had been paying my way through graduate school at CSU with a lawn mowing business and so we decided that it was time to sell that business and move closer to our new investment. After about a month, we sold our house and business and moved to the town of Agate, CO. This was about 20 miles from the park and I thought it was a good buffer zone.

We proceeded to work on the park and after about a year it was starting to bring in enough of an income to cover the credit card payments and the mortgages. At that time we still had good credit… just a lot of it. We owed about 100k in credit cards so it was time to find a bank to refinance the park and pay off these debts. I think I tried about 20 banks before I finally found one that would do the deal. I was able to refinance, pay off the credit cards, and had a good interest rate and 20 year loan with a payment of about $1,000 less than what it was before.

All of a sudden, I had some money (credit) again and was ready to do it all over again. There was another park in Fort Morgan, CO that just came on the market and seemed to be a good fit. This park had about 50 Mobile Home and 50 RV spaces. So about a month later, I was at the bank again maxing out my credit cards to the tune of $80,000 and was the proud owner of another Mobile Home and RV Park. This park had an out of state owner who was being robbed by his managers to the tune of about $3,000 per month. He had a great income as a pilot and didn't have the time to worry about the park. It was basically just a write off.

I knew that this park was going to need a large time commitment at first so I packed up my family and we moved to the park. It was an old KOA and had an apartment above the office. Anyway, I moved my wife and 2 boys to the park in September and then about a month later, we had a husband and wife that had been staying in the RV park come into the office one day and make us an offer of about $150,000 more for the park than we had paid the previous month. That was an easy decision and a quick closing. We moved to the park in September and had moved back to the Limon area by the end of October with our credit cards paid off and about $100,000 in the bank. This is when I knew that I had found my calling. I was going to be buying Mobile Home and RV Parks for a long time.

One of the things that I noticed while operating the park in Fort Morgan for that one month period was that operating an overnight RV Park was much more time intensive and more like a business as compared to the Mobile Home portion. I enjoyed meeting so many new people with different backgrounds and stories and saw how this could be a very rewarding experience for someone wanting to make a career change and become involved in this industry. It was just more labor and time intensive.

Through the purchase of the second park in Fort Morgan I met a broker that had been specializing in selling Mobile Home, RV Parks and Motels for the past 30 years. I decided I should get my real estate license so I could start making money selling parks that I did not want to buy. I became licensed in several states under this broker, Carl Smeltzer, and started my brokerage career.

About this same time, I discovered a website on the internet that had the domain name of www.themobilehomeparkstore.com. I started watching the site, placed my brokerage listings on the site and began driving all over the Midwest looking at the Mobile Home Parks for sale that were listed. I was having some success in getting leads from the site and thought it was a great concept.

Then one day I went to the site and it wasn't there anymore. I tried the next day and the next and still no site. I was able to get in touch with site owner a few days later and asked him what was up. He said he was moving and was going into ministry and did not have any interest in the site. I asked him if he would sell the domain name to me and if I remember right he said I could basically name my price. I think we settled on one thousand dollars and all of a sudden I had an internet site that I had no idea on how to run.

He told me what software to buy and walked me through getting things setup and that was the beginning of MobileHomeParkStore. com. When the previous owner had run the site, he was basically working a few states and getting commissions on parks that were sold as a direct result of the site. I think one of the things that frustrated him was that he was not getting credit for many of the sales and was not making anything from it. I decided to do things differently and just charge a nominal fee to individuals and brokers and become basically the nationwide MLS for Mobile Home Parks for Sale.

A few months later, I was noticing that many brokers that sold mobile home parks also sold RV parks and many investors were looking for either mobile home or RV parks. It was shortly thereafter, that I started the website RVParkStore.com as an exact replica of the mobile home park site, but for RV Parks.

Being involved with these web sites for the past 9 years has been a learning experience like no other. I would guess that we have helped individuals and brokers sell over 2,000 Mobile Home and RV Parks and many parks have been sold several times on the site.

On my first 2 MH/RV Park deals, I was very lucky. I spent about 30 minutes of due diligence on the first park and a few hours on the second park. It would not be until some of my future Park investments that not doing proper due diligence would come back to haunt me. I was very lucky. Don't ever take the Due Diligence step lightly! Even paying someone a couple of thousand dollars to help you in this process will be one of the best insurance policies you can ever get. In fact, they will probably find some things that you should go back to the seller with and renegotiate. In many cases, hiring someone to help you with this process will not only save you money down the road but also help you reduce the purchase price or down payment.

Since that time, I have purchased over 35 Mobile Home and RV Parks and currently own 9 parks. In addition, while I was working as a broker I was involved in another 10+ RV Park sales and have helped over a thousand buyers and sellers through RVParkStore. com.

Many times I will refer to my experiences with mobile home parks as well. In doing so, these concepts will apply to RV Parks and Campgrounds in one way or another. In addition, I will discuss the major differences and similarities between investing in Mobile Home Parks vs RV Parks and Campgrounds.

As I have continued to buy, manage, fix up, and sell parks I made some great purchases but also made many mistakes. The purpose of this book is to educate you on the process of buying an RV Park or Campground as well as teach you what to look out for and learn from my mistakes.

Definitions and Terminology:

What is an RV Park?

RV Parks are basically tracts of land that have two or more spaces/sites that provide for occupancy for one of the many types of Recreational Vehicles. Many times you hear the terms RV Park or Campground used interchangeably. However, RV Parks are just that, for Recreational Vehicles and Campgrounds are for those setting up Camp – whether they walk-in, drive-in, or arrive by other means such as horseback or ATV. In many cases, a facility will be a combination of RV Park and Campground.

There are several different types of Facilities:

- **Primitive** – these types of RV Parks / Campgrounds have no facilities or conveniences. They are basically just a tract of land with several spaces cleared and leveled out for tents or recreational vehicles. Bring your generator and firewood.

- **Partially Developed** – these types of campgrounds may have bathrooms, and larger spaces. Some of the spaces may have water and electric but typically not individual sewer.

- **Developed** – these are campgrounds in which most of the spaces have water, sewer, and electric hookups. In many cases, these facilities have additional services such as cable tv and wifi service available as well.

- We will focus on this third type of RV Park and variations thereof. However, in many cases, an RV Park or campground will be comprised of several different sections/areas. There may be a fully developed section, a partially developed area, as well as a primitive/tenting area.

RV Parks can be further classified into the type or purpose they serve. These include the overnight park, the destination overnight park, the destination resort park, the seasonal park, and the extended stay park, the membership park, and the coop/condo parks.

- **Overnight RV Parks** – the overnight type RV parks are those that are usually just a stopover for an RV'er to get to where they are going. Like a Motel just off the interstate they are a place to pull off and get a good nights rest before continuing on your journey. Usually the biggest key to the overnight type parks success is LOCATION. Most of these parks are located just off the interstate or major highway. The people that will be staying here want to pull in, hookup, eat, check their email, watch tv, and go to bed. If they have kids, then a swimming pool may be a nice attraction. It is usually more important to have good access and signage in this type of park than it is to load up on amenities, etc. After all, your customers will only be there for one or two days.

- **Destination Overnight RV Parks** – this type of RV Park is typically located near another major attraction and thereby gets most of its business because of that attraction. For example, an RV Park near Mount Rushmore or Yellowstone National Park.

- **Destination Resort RV Parks** – while these types of parks are often located nearby a major attraction such as in Destination Overnight RV Parks, these parks often turn into being more of the destination itself. These types of parks are becoming popular for RV'ers of all ages and offer activities for the young and older crowd. With shuffleboard, waterslides, marinas, fishing, and dancing and entertainment, these type of parks aim to keep people entertained without having to leave the property.

- **Extended Stay RV Parks** – these types of parks are similar in many ways to a mobile home park in that the occupants are there for more than one month or even permanently. In many cases, mobile home parks allow RVer's to rent a space just as a mobile home owner would do. (Word of Caution: when buying a park that has permanent RV's check on the zoning to make sure it is legal to have an RV renting a space as the mobile home owners do. I have seen some instances in which an RV may only occupy a space for up to 30 days, 180 days, etc.) As the price of housing goes up, many couples or single adults have opted to moving into an RV in one of these types of parks.

- **Seasonal RV Parks** – we have all heard of "snowbirds" and seasonal RV parks have become popular due to these "snowbirds". In Texas, refer to them as "winter Texans". These type of parks have very little occupancy during the summer months and then as it gets colder up north, the snowbirds (RV'ers) drive south for the winter. Popular areas for these types of parks are Florida, Arizona, South Texas, and similar areas. It is the RVer's home away from home and many times they rent the same space year after year.   Rent is collected either monthly, seasonally, or annually. In addition to the parks that people go to in the winter, there are those parks that people visit in the summer. Whether it is in Ohio, Colorado, Wisconsin, or other popular summer getaways many RVers have a summer RVing home and a winter one.

◐ We owned an RV Park in Arizona and one in Washington in which we sold lots. During the winter our salesman (broker) and a few others on our staff would sell lots in Arizona and then move up to Washington and do the same thing in the summer. It worked amazingly and we sold many lots in Washington to those that bought lots in Arizona.

- **Membership RV Parks** – membership parks are those parks in which the park sells memberships to the RV owners and they in turn have a right to stay in the park and use its facilities for free or discounted rates for a limited or unlimited amount of time. Blue Mesa Ranch RV Resort is one of these Membership type parks. When you purchase a membership from a park such as this, you typically have several options with your purchase such as buying the right to use their affiliated parks for free or at a discounted rate. In most cases, when you buy into a membership park, you will pay from $2,000 to $10,000 and then have dues every year in the $200-$400 range. You will then be allowed to stay there usually for up to 14 days per month and use their facilities. The membership parks make their money from the sale of these memberships and they may be able to sell 10 memberships for every available space. If you do the math and are able to sell 10 memberships for $5,000 per space you would be grossing $50,000 per space. Most RV parks can be built for under $10,000 per lot.

- **RV Park Subdivisions or Coops** – these type of RV Parks are often located in the same areas as the seasonal RV parks but instead of renting a space by the month or year, you either purchase a share of stock and a have a long term renewable lease to use and improve that lot (coop) or purchase a lot (subdivision) and park your RV or Park Model here as a second home. In both of these types of parks, there is usually a yearly maintenance or subdivision fee to cover the common operational expenses. These types of parks are becoming increasingly popular as it gives the RV owners the right to own the land and avoid the ever increasing monthly rents.

- **Franchise Parks** – these are those RV Parks that are owned by private individuals and companies but are part of a Franchise – such as KOA and Yogi Bear's. These parks can be Overnight or Destination style parks and when purchasing this type of park, it is important to consider the franchise fees that you will be paying as well as the advertising you will be getting as part of that franchise fee.

There are approximately 12,500 RV parks and campgrounds in the United States and according to our lists, the states with the most RV Parks in order are:

California, Florida, Texas, and Michigan, and the state with the fewest is:

Hawaii – I do not know of any RV Parks in Hawaii (there may be some campgrounds there though).

What is a Recreational Vehicle?

A recreational vehicle comes in many shapes, sizes, and types. They include pull behind campers, tent trailers, van conversions, fifth wheels, motorhomes and the million dollar bus conversions we see on TV.

RV's can be categorized as either Motorized or Towable

Motorized RV Types

Class A Motorhomes - these are those units that are typically described as Motorhomes. They are typically over 15,000 pounds and from 30 to 40 feet long with one or more slideouts. They are literally a home on wheels. The price tag on these are usually from $75,000 and up into the several hundreds of thousands of dollars. Class A Motorhomes also includes the Custom Bus Conversions, the large and luxurious and customized coaches which can range from over a half million to well over a million dollars.

Class B Motorhomes - these are often referred to as "Van Conversions" and are the smallest of the three classes. They basically use the standard van body with basic amenities and are ideal for 1 or 2 people for a few nights or so. They typically are in the $50,000 range and are from 16 to 20 feet long.

Class C Motorhomes - they are often referred to as to as mini-motorhomes. These typically have the same type of drivers seat of a van but then also have a sleeping area above the cab and then a box behind the cab. They typically are in the 25 to 35 feet range and cost in the range of $50,000 to $135,000.

RV's that are Towed

Travel Trailers - these come in a variety of sizes and can range from the simple model costing about $10,000 all the way up to those models that resemble the Class A Motorhomes without the engine for $60,000. They are hitched at the rear of the pulling vehicle and depending on their size and weight, may be towed by the standard size car or will require a suburban or heavy duty truck.

Fifth-Wheel Trailers - they also come in a variety of sizes with different amenities. However, they are different in that they are pulled by a pickup truck with a hitch in the bed of the truck. There are also heavy duty trucks designed specifically to pull the larger fifth wheel trailers. Fifth-Wheels have an extension over the tow vehicle which usually houses the master bedroom. These types of trailers are much easier to pull since the load is in the center of the tow vehicle rather than behind it. They are also easier to back up and turn. They range in price from $15,000 up to $150,000 and can be in the 20 to 40 foot long range.

Tent Trailer or Folding Trailers - these are usually the most economical choice and popular with families that are just starting out with an RV. They range from around $5,000 to $25,000 and are typically lightweight and able to be pulled by standard cars, small trucks, and SUV's. They usually can sleep up to 6 people and have basic amenities. They can be taken down or setup quickly. I owned a nice model for a few years and the only thing I did not like about it was that when you fold it up, there is very little storage as compared to the other RV's I have owned.

Truck Campers - these are the type of campers that fit into the bed of your pickup truck. They are made to fit into most trucks, small and large. They typically have a small living space but are ideal for taking off road with a 4 wheel drive or just taking a weekend camping trip. They typically range fro $7,500 to $30,000 with the more expensive models offering more amenities and even slideouts.

Park Models – they are 400 square foot movable resort cottages that look like a small and upscale mobile home and have very basic features to elaborate décor. They are typically in the $40,000 to $50,000 range.

Differences between buying a Mobile Home vs RV Park: When considering the purchase of a mobile home park as compared to an RV park there are many factors to consider. While mobile home parks and RV parks are often sold by the same brokers and are combined in one facility, they are not the same and both require different amounts and types of management. The following comparisons are for Overnight/Destination RV parks as compared to the typical mobile home park in which the lots are rented out on a monthly basis. In many cases, the seasonal or extended stay RV parks will have more of the qualities of the typical mobile home park rather than those of the Overnight/Destination type RV parks.

Length of Stay: Mobile Home owners are in the park permanently or at least until they sell their home and move somewhere else. RVer's are in the park for usually a week or less. The longer a home or resident stays in the park, the more likely it will have the qualities of a mobile home park and the less time a home or resident stays in the park, the more likely it will resemble the operations of an RV park.

Management: This is probably one of the most significant differences between RV and mobile home parks. In most cases, it takes less time and manpower to run a mobile home park than an RV park. There are several factors for this:

- With a mobile home park, the manager will typically see the residents of each space only once per month when the rent is paid and anytime there is a problem. However, with an RV Park you may have a new camper in the space every day or every few days. You may have to acquaint them with the park, the facilities, and in many cases the area. How to get here or there, where to eat, etc.

- In addition, many RV parks will have showers and restrooms that need to be cleaned several times during the day. Most mobile home owners have their own showers and toilets.

- In Mobile Home Parks, the manager usually only maintains the common areas and the residents maintain their own spaces, etc. However, in an RV Park, the manager will not only maintain the common areas, but should check each space to make sure it is clean before renting. As before, these spots may have a different RV'er each day and so it is ongoing.

Ease of Movement: While it will cost an owner of a mobile home 1-2 thousand dollars or more to move their mobile home out of the park and set it up somewhere else, the owner of an Recreational Vehicle can hook up, move and reset their RV up in another park in a couple of hours or less and for the cost of gas. Thus, you have to work much harder at keeping the RV'er satisfied with the park if you want to keep them there.

Eviction: In a mobile home park if you have someone that is not paying rent or causing other problems, you will have to go to court and deal with the judges and it may take several weeks to have them evicted out of the park. However, in an RV Park, the rent is usually paid in advance and if it is not paid, you should be able to have the RV removed immediately for lack of payment or other issues. These laws differ from state to state so make sure to check first to stay legal.

Rent Control: RV parks owners are not typically subject to rent control ordinances as are mobile home park owners.

Utilities: In a typical mobile home park the park owner will generally only pay the utilities for any common areas and buildings as well as for street lights. The individual mobile home owners will pay for their own gas, electric, water, sewer, cable, and internet. However, in an RV Park, this is all bundled up in a nightly or weekly rate and that rate should be adjusted to include all these utilities and amenities. You might shudder when a big 40' rig pulls in the middle of July and powers up a couple of a/c units after plugging into your electric pedestal.

Other Improvements: While both RV & MH parks will have the homesites, utilities, roads, it is common for RV parks to also have a store, recreational hall, and restrooms and showers. In addition, a higher percentage of RV parks compared to MH parks will have a swimming pool and other recreational facilities such as shuffleboard, basketball, and video games. What this will equate to is once again, more management time and energy. An RV Park of 400 spaces will probably have two to three times more employees than a comparably sized mobile home park.

Taxes: Just like the taxes you pay when you stay at a motel, you will pay taxes to stay in an RV park. Usually the only way around the lodging/transient tax is to stay for 30 days or more. The residents in a mobile home park are not subject to this type of tax. They are just subject to the yearly mobile home taxes to the county treasurer. The park owner will pay the taxes on the land (dirt and improvements) for both MH & RV parks.

Capitalization Rate: Typically a mobile home park will sell at a lower cap rate than an RV park. There are always exceptions but this is the general rule. If a mobile home park is selling at a cap rate of 10% then an RV park in that same market area will typically be selling for a 11-13% cap rate. Smaller RV parks generally sell for higher cap rates than do larger ones. Destination and overnight style RV parks are generally priced at higher cap rates than the extended stay and seasonal type RV parks. Also, parks that are rated higher by Woodalls or any type of star ratings will generally sell for more $$$ (a smaller cap rate).

Finding a Park to Buy: In my experiences as a broker, investor and by running the Mobile Home Park Website as well as the RV Park Website for many years, I have noticed that there are usually five times or more buyers out there looking for Mobile Home Parks than there are for RV Parks. What this equates to for the RV Park Investor, is that there is a better inventory of potential RV Parks to purchase as well as less competition. I have seen some very good RV Parks sit on the website for a few months and wonder why they have not sold. There are Great Opportunities out there especially if you are not set on one particular area.

Long Distance Ownership: Mobile Home Parks are often owned by individuals or companies that do not live in the same city or state where the park is located. They hire an onsite manager and visit a couple of times per year. However, with an RV Park, most owners live at the park or nearby and are involved with the management of the park on a day to day basis. It is possible to run an RV Park from a distance but in order to do so you have to really trust your manager and other staff. As I mentioned earlier with the park in

Fort Morgan, Colorado, the managers that were running the park when I purchased it were keeping over half of the overnight RV income for themselves. I also heard a story from another investor that owned an RV Park about 300 miles from his home. If he started to distrust his managers about the number of RVer's that were staying in the park, he would drive to the park in a car that the managers did not know and count the RV's in the park. He would then call from his cell phone and ask how many RV's were there. They would usually lie and then he would pull into the office and have them walk around the park with him. After they started making excuses, they would be fired on the spot. He would then have to find a new manager and train them and it really became a burden for him. After 4 different managers in 2 years, he and his family decided to sell their home and run the park themselves. He enjoyed the experience and the park is very profitable today.

Financing: It is usually harder to obtain a loan for an RV park than a mobile home park and that is one reason why a higher percentage of owners offer to seller finance RV Parks as compared to Mobile Home Parks. When seeking financing on an RV park, you will be typically obtaining a loan with interest rates a point or two higher than that of a mobile home park. For many types of investment properties, the loan is based on the property more so than the purchaser. However, with an RV Park, the loan is not only based on the property itself, but also the borrower's credit and experience in running similar types of businesses. It often helps to have a well drafted business plan when applying for financing.

Who is Going to Stay at the Park?

RV parks will generally have several different types of customers and the park owner and manager will need to recognize this in order to open up additional opportunities and maximize the current ones.

- *Family Campers* - this category is made up of the families that take one or several short weekend trips and maybe one or two longer trips per year during the summer or other school breaks. This number has been increasing rapidly as families have realized that it is cheaper to travel vian RV and cook their meals in the RV than take a car, stay in motels, and eat every meal at restaurants.

- *Part-timers* - this would include many of the retired or semi-retired people that may spend a month or two on the road going from one destination to another.

- *Full-timers* - these are the people that sold their house and live in their RV year round. They may stay in one park for a few months and then stay in 10 different parks in 10 nights. They have the freedom to pull up and move their home whenever they want a change or want to see something new.

- *RV Club Members* - these people have typically purchased a membership in one of the popular RV park clubs and are attracted to parks that recognize that affiliation and offer discounted rates. Coast-to-Coast and Good Sam's are these types of clubs.

- *Snowbirds* - these people typically have a home up north and head south for the winter. The snowbird population has exploded and owning a park that caters to this crowd can be very profitable.

- *Other types* - many people have their main home but use their RV for temporary housing. Many construction and similar type jobs require you to take up lodging near the job site and many workers bring an RV instead of commuting or staying in local motels. Once again they can save money on lodging and food.

Types of RV Sites:

- *Pull Through* – these have become more common as the size of the typical RV continues to increase. It is much easier to pull one of those big rigs straight through a space.

- *Back In* – these are basically those spaces that you back the RV in and out of. Depending on the length and width of the space, the width of the road and the size of the RV this can either be a simple process or a nightmare.

- *Group Spaces* – these are typically large sites or a cluster of sites intended for several families, friends, or other groups.

- *Full Hookup* – spaces that are full hookup will include water, sewer, electric and often will include cable and telephone.

- *Partial Hookup* - these will usually have water and electric but no sewer. Sometimes they will include water only.

- *Dry* – these spaces are just designated parking spaces for the most part.

Why Invest in RV Parks:

When deciding to invest in any type of real estate, stock investment, or any other type of investment whether a CD or an oil well, these all include with them a risk however small or large. Depending on the risk you perceive in each type of investment you will expect or hope for a certain return. As the perceived risk goes up you will want a greater potential return and vice versa.

According to most books and advice you get from investment advisors, real estate usually is regarded as being a safe investment as the downturns in real estate have usually been short-lived and have corrected themselves quickly. This is generally speaking and goes for most real estate markets. However, when you invest in markets that have one major employer or are dependent on a certain industry, you may run the risk of a long term decline in values and occupancy if something happens to that employer or industry.

Like most investment real estate, RV Parks and Campgrounds are similar in that you typically expect them to increase in value, produce an increasing monthly cash flow as the rates and number of RVer's on the road increase, have income tax advantages, and include an increase in equity as you pay down the debt. However, more so for RV Parks than other investment real estate, the management of the park is critical. Your investment will often depend on repeat business and referrals and if you are not taking care of your guests, they will not come back.

Buying an RV park has some similarities to other types of real estate investments but also has many similarities to businesses. Most people decide to go into business for themselves for the following reasons:

- They want to become the boss and be in control of their success or failure

- They feel like they can set work at their own schedule – freedom from the 9-5 monotony.

- They feel like they have many skills that they would like to use that they are not currently using.

- They feel like they can make more money than staying in their current job.

- They are looking to either replace or supplement their current income.

Advantages of purchasing/owning an RV Park as compared to other investment real estate:

1. Most RV Parks are more resistant to recessions than many other types of businesses and real estate investments. A high percentage of RVer's are retired or semi retired and traveling across the country is one of the most affordable means of travel. In addition these RVer's typically have enough income to ride the ups and downs of the economy. Fuel prices have not even deterred the majority of RV owners.

2. The number of RV's being sold continues to increase and the demand for sites for those RV's to park either for one night or several should also increase proportionally. One of the major factors is that baby boomers are reaching their prime age ranges and are buying RV's. They represent the largest percentage of RV ownership rates. According to the Recreational Vehicle Industry Association, more RVs were shipped in the first six months of 2006 than in any other during the past 33 years. A total of nearly 225,000 RVs! In addition, according to RV industry forecaster Dr. Richard Curtin, director of surveys at the University of Michigan, he projects that the number of RV owning households will rise to 8.2 percent by 2010.

3. Seasonal RV Parks and Extended Stay style RV parks exist in a large part to provide affordable housing - there has always been and will always be a need for affordable housing. These types of RV Parks are just that.

4. Like owning and operating a motel, bed & breakfast, or similar lodging business, owning an RV Park and Campground can be a fun, exciting and profitable family operation. You will meet people from all different backgrounds and areas of the country. However, one of the biggest advantages with RV Parks and Campgrounds is that you are renting out the land and utility hookups. You may have to pick up some trash here and there but you will not have to clean the rooms every day, replace carpet and paint every couple of years. There is only so much damage that someone can do to the dirt. There are many more ways a motel or similar type facility can be damaged.

5. Consider how many people flock to the many coastlines to take advantage of the beaches and ocean views. In the unfortunate event that a hurricane or other natural disaster hits this resort area, it is likely to do much more damage to the hotels, condos, restaurants, and other service businesses in that area. As an owner of an RV Park in that area, you will usually sustain much less damage and can be renting out your spaces much faster than if you had owned one of those other resort properties that now has to be completely rebuilt. In addition, as an owner of an RV Park in that area, your land value is often worth more than the value of the RV Park Business itself and can offer a more lucrative exit strategy should you decide to sell to a developer.

6. The operating expenses for a typical RV park will typically run between 45-50 percent while the expenses for a typical motel will often be 10% percent higher. For the most part, this is again due to the fact that you are not responsible for painting, cleaning carpets, fixing windows, and all the fun jobs of the motel / apartment maintenance personnel. You are typically only responsible up to where the RV connects to your utilities and the maintenance of the common areas.

7. As far as depreciation, motels and apartments have a large value attributable to the building itself and the building portion is generally required to be depreciated over 27.5 years However, for RV Parks, the depreciable costs are typically the roads, water lines, sewer lines, electric poles and so on. These are considered land improvements and are typically depreciated over a period of 15 years. This increased depreciation over the first 15 years is a major tax benefit for many investors.

8. Another hidden benefit of RV Parks is the barriers to entry for competition. In many areas of the country, it is difficult to get the proper zoning, meet all the local, state, and federal requirements to build a new community and actually make a profit. Face it, once you get all the permits and licenses and have the curbs, roads, driveways, utilities, pads and everything else built out, you will have a carrying cost until you actually get the word out that you are open and people start finding you.

   State and local governments restrict new RV Park developments for many reasons, such as existing park owners allowing the park to deteriorate, and less property tax base to fund schools, police, fire, and other government services.

In addition to the limited number of new RV Parks being built, many of the existing RV Parks are being sold for other development purposes (townhomes, condos, beach houses, etc). Many of these RV parks were built in resort type areas or just on the outskirts of the cities they are located in. Now the cities or other developments have grown around these older RV parks and the land is much more valuable to the developers than to keep the property an RV Park.

9.   Another benefit of RV Parks is that in most cases you have individuals that own their own RV's and will tend to take care of the RV as well as their lot. Since you are renting the land and the utility connections, there is not near as many things that your renters can do to cost you major repairs. Sure they may flush things down the sewer and let the water run, but they will not be putting holes in the walls and floors or spilling things on the carpet as they will in your apartment rentals. You rent out the land and do not have to fix leaky kitchen faucets or toilets.

Types of RV Parks to Consider:

When deciding on investing in an RV Park you can either build a new park or else buy an existing park. While they both have advantages and disadvantages I would encourage you to go with an existing park first so that you may gain experience in the industry. One reason why is that an existing park has a proven track record whereas a new park has no track record. You are hoping there is a need and no matter how many studies you do your success cannot be measured until the park is open and marketing is in place. In addition, with an existing park you should be making money from day one if you buy it right. With a new development, it will usually take a year minimum before you start bringing in any revenue whatsoever. Also, with existing parks you can usually obtain financing (owner or bank) whereas you will have a hard time obtaining financing for a new development. A final reason I recommend an existing park is that you can often receive training from the seller in order to get you going. With a new development you do not receive this training.

To expand further, you can basically look at four different types:

1. ***Building a New Park -*** this is starting from scratch and will take time, money, and patience. This is usually the riskiest and drawn out option but can potentially be a great opportunity. Many of the new RV Parks being built are the seasonal ones or those that sell deeded lots or shares in a coop.

2. ***Buying an Established and Successful Park -*** this could include any of the different types of RV Parks (overnight, seasonal, destination, etc.). These parks are on the map and well taken care of and are ready for you to step in and take over. You are buying a cash flow that should increase as rates increase over time. You will pay a premium price for this type of park.

3. ***Buying an Existing Park that is not to its Potential -*** this is the type of park that has the basic framework set, but it not being run efficiently or as profitably as it could be with minor changes. Things such as making the entrance and signs attractive, advertising in the right places, having proper night lighting, and offering the services that the campers being targeted expect, can do wonders to increase business and your bottom line. For example, take an RV park that is off the interstate in a great location but does not do any OR the

right type of advertising on the highway. I had an RV park that was listed in Trailer Life and Woodall's and many other places but unless the RVer knew when to pull off, they would miss it. The park was right off the interstate but could not be seen by the traffic until it was too late. We had the State Highway Dept install one of those little blue signs going in each direction on the interstate (it was a one time fee of about $200 per sign). We had about 70 spaces and during the season we were typically filling about 20 of those spaces. However, after those new signs were installed our traffic more than doubled. Leasing some billboard space 20-50 miles down the road in both directions might have also been a good idea in order to prepare these people to stop. In the last several years I have driven several hundred thousand miles up and down the highways throughout much of the U.S. looking at Mobile Home and RV Parks to purchase as well as visit the properties I owned at the time. My travel plans were usually to drive until I was tired so I could get home as soon as possible. Many times when I would start to get tired I would be nearing a city that had several motels. One of the most effective billboard placement strategies I have ever seen is when you are pulling into a city and see a billboard that is advertising a motel 50 miles down the road. If you are like me, I would much rather make 50 more miles that day before stopping. I think this would also be a great advertising tool for RV Parks and Campgrounds. "Get them to go the extra Mile".

In these types of parks you want to buy them based on the current income and expenses and then increase the value and profitability by addressing these minor issues that the previous owner has neglected to do. When buying RV or Mobile Home parks or any other real estate, these are the type of properties I am on the lookout for.

4. ***Buying a Turnaround Park*** **-** this is the type of RV Park that is a mess. Everything that should be being done is not. The park will have very little or no traffic or may not be operating at all. You are not buying this park because of the income it is currently generating but rather based on your anticipated income after you fix all the problems. This type of investment usually has the best potential to increase in value for existing parks but will take the most time, money, and efforts. Make sure that the extra time and efforts will be worth it. Turnaround parks are often priced at less than replacement cost as the owner may have lost interest or is having financial difficulties. The two major factors to look at here are what it will cost to fix the park up and once this is done whether or not the park has a location sufficient to have the desired occupancy.

Size of RV Park to Purchase:

Most of the multiple RV Park investors are looking to purchase parks that are in the 200+ site range and so the competition as well as the prices will generally be higher. For your first park, I would suggest you focus on the parks that are in the 25 to 200 space range. Typically the larger the park, the more potential profits there will be. However in many cases the smaller parks with higher occupancy will generate more income and net profits per space. You will need to take this on a case by case basis. Other factors to consider will be the additional income streams that the park may have now or could be implemented in the future.

Any size of park can be run efficiently and profitably as long as there is a good market for that park.

When deciding what type of park to buy, you need to decide on your investment goals, evaluate the amount of time you have, talk to others in the business about the time requirements for your potential purchase and then begin your search for parks that will fit within those goals. Make sure your goals are reasonable. It is not likely your are going to buy a 100 space park in a good market operating well for a 20 cap and it is not likely you will find a park operating well in a good market that will be purchased for no money down, etc.

Where to Find RV Parks to Buy:

When starting your search to buy an RV Park there are several ways to do this. I would suggest trying each of these as they will all give you a different perspective and offer comparables to evaluate. Then when you find the park that seems to fit, you will have the knowledge and be able to move quickly. If you wait too long, you will most likely find out it is under contact. So it is best to be ready when the time comes.

When you are searching for an RV Park to purchase, it is often the park or deal that is least advertised or that is new on the market that may represent the best deals. But don't forget about those parks that have been on the market for a long time. You never know when the seller will come to terms.

Owners become Sellers for many reasons which include:

- Death
- Divorce

- Partnership Breakups

- Bankruptcy

- Buying or Trading Up

- Moving

- Tired of the Business

- Retiring

- Poor Health

Here are a several potential ways to find properties:

1. *RVParkStore.com:* On average we are adding over 30 new properties for sale to the website each and every month. We have really been marketing this site to increase the traffic and listings and if you have been watching the site for a few months you will have noticed the changes. Of these new listings, I would estimate that about 40% of them are reasonably priced and will sell quickly. About 30% of the listings are borderline and may sit on the site for a few months but will sell within 6 months to a year. The other 30% are overpriced and/or not currently viable projects due to a bad local market or other factors. It is the first 40% that most of you will be looking for. The best way to stay updated on new properties for sale is to join our investor list. You receive all the new listings by email. As soon as we receive the listing, it is immediately sent out to this list of investors.

   The benefits of being on the investor list is twofold: one you get emailed all the listings and you start seeing what price RV Parks are listed for and can usually tell which parks are worth following up on quickly. The other benefit is that you will see the listings in your email inbox and not forget to check for them on a regular basis. .

2. ***Other Websites:*** Loopnet.com, CIMLS.com, Real Estate Company Websites, Business Brokerage Websites, and numerous other similar sites: It is not uncommon to find those sellers that do not know the best places to market their RV Parks or Campgrounds for sale and you may find them in off the wall places (be sure to tell them about RVParkStore. com!). It is worth checking out some of these other websites that do not have a big RV Park investor following.

3. ***Google Web Searches:*** We are always doing these searches looking for new RV Parks and Campgrounds for sale to promote RVParkStore.com to. Every once in a while there will be a good potential deal listed for sale down about 20 or 30 pages in the search results.

4. ***Contact Real Estate Brokers*** that specialize in selling RV Parks. These are the professionals that are out there every day trying to get parks listed for sale and will often have pocket listings or listings that they cannot otherwise advertise. I would contact any broker that does business in areas you are looking and be very specific about what you are looking for. It is good to stay in touch with them on a regular basis so when they get a new listing they will think about you if it meets your criteria. Here is a list of Brokers to contact:

Company Name	Contact Name	Phone	Market Served
Parks and Places	.	616-301-0765	Entire US
NAI Rio Grande Valley	Pauline Zurovec	956-425-9400	Texas
Five Star Realty	Patsy Archer	907-252-7373	Alaska
The Brokerage Real Estate	Steven L. Weinberg	800-945-0255	Colorado
Realty Sales Realty Sales	Brian Solum	218-751-1177	MN, SD, Ontario

Company Name	Contact Name	Phone	Market Served
Trimble Private Brokerage	George MacLeod	207-944-8771	Maine
LHP Realty, LLC	David Koscielecki	928-854-5477	Arizona
Pinon Real Estate Group	Julie Kersting	719-395-0200	Colorado
EWM Realtors	Mike Hindle	954-655-6447	Florida
Darrell Hess & Associates	Darrell Hess	828-452-1535	Southeast
Recreational Investments	Morgan Davis	512-328-8004	TX, NM, FL, AZ
Nadine World Real Estate	Nadine World	541-689-8296	Oregon
Baehre Real Estate	Russell Baehre	830-896-5050	Texas
McCarty Real Estate	Roxie McCarty Jona Vacek	903-586-3144 972-743-5926	Texas
Equitable Management Co.	Barry Henson	770-579-6777 Ext 108	Southeast - TX to NC

5. *Contact other Real Estate Brokers* that are in areas that you are looking for properties. It is amazing how many RV Parks are listed by brokers that have no idea how to value a park, how to market a park for sale, and where to find a buyer for the park. If you are looking for an RV Park for sale in a certain state or city, I would find all the brokers you can in these areas and send them an email asking them if they have any RV Parks for sale or if they know of any. The ones that reply to you with an offer to keep an eye out for you will be the ones that you will follow up with on a regular basis.

6. *Direct Mail:* I have been using this method in various forms over the years and have purchased many Mobile Home and RV Parks this way. In setting up your direct mail campaign, you will want to set yourself apart from the other companies and individuals that send out mail to the park owners/managers. Here are just a few ideas that I have used in the past:

a) Make your mailing piece stand out from the rest of the competitors.

b) Identify yourself as a real person, not some LLC without an identity.

c) Incorporate useful information in the mailing so that it will be retained by the owner. I continue to get calls from mailings I sent out several years ago from owners that kept my postcard.

d) Possibly include magnets, notepads, or other useful gadgets with your phone number on them that will be right in front of the owner when they decide to sell. My favorite is mouse pads.

e) In addition, any direct mail campaign should include more than one contact to each recipient. Anywhere from 3-5 contacts per year should be made in order to keep you and your company in front of the potential sellers. I like to switch it up by varying the mailings to include different letters, postcards, etc so it is not the same piece each and every time.

Another important part of the direct mail process is that you have to get a good list of prospects with which to mail to. The best way to do this is to purchase an existing list like the one we have on our site or with a list service such as infousa.com and then work on building it to fit your needs.

7. **Cold Calling:** Basically you can go to our website, RVPark-Store.com and go to the park directory and start making phone calls to parks that are in the areas you are looking. I have found it best to identify yourself as someone that is looking to purchase an RV Park in that area and were won-

dering if this park is for sale or if they know of one for sale. You will get hang-ups and occasionally even be yelled at, but for the most part people will be sociable. Many times these owners/managers will know of other parks for sale in the area. It is often good to follow up by mail with anyone that seems to be a potential prospect in the future.

8. ***Major Newspapers, Recreational Vehicle and Camping Magazines.*** Just like staying on top of listings on RVParkStore.com you will need to stay on top of these classified ads to be sure you don't miss potential deals that will be snatched up by other investors. Many of the larger newspapers have an online service that will allow you to sign up to be emailed listings that match particular criteria.

9. ***Driving through potential parks:*** If you see a park that looks interesting, take a drive through, stop and talk to the owner/manager, leave your card, and if it seems to be a good fit, follow up on a regular basis. If you make a good impression on the owner and stop in routinely just to see how things are going without being pushy, you will likely be called first when the owner is ready to sell. Don't bother the residents though as you will often upset the manager and owner and they will not be open to talking with you.

10. ***Visit Industry Trade Shows and Similar Events:*** You will make many great contacts with other investors and industry professionals, and will start to develop a network of people that will help you in your search and management of your RV Park investment.

11. ***Subscribe to RSS feeds or Google Alerts*** to get news on RV Parks that are in the news. You will be looking for parks and

park owners that are in trouble. Many times, the owner is not in compliance, behind on bills, or is doing something to stir up a ruckus with the residents. This is a great way to find motivated sellers especially if you have a solution to their problem. Make sure that you have a good solution to the problem so you don't end up in the same boat as the seller.

12. **County Tax Records:** Most counties have a listing of the RV Parks in the county and some information in regards to the owners, etc. By searching the country records you might also be able to see what the park was last sold at, is currently valued at by the county (which is often quite low) and whether the taxes are paid. If the taxes are not paid, this may indicate a motivated seller.

13. **Contact appraisers, banks, title companies,** friends, relatives and let them know what you are looking for and to keep their eye open. Offer them a finder's fee if they find something that you end up purchasing.

14. **Heirs:** Another great place to buy a park. They usually want cash not an RV Park to manage.

15. **Make Unsolicited Offers:** In the past, I have collected information on certain Mobile Home and RV Parks, number of spaces, rents, occupancy, who pays water, sewer, and trash and then plugged this into a basic valuation formula and generated offers. I would prepare a purchase and sale contract with all the standard provisions with the price I was willing to pay and mail these out to the owners. I received a much higher response rate doing this than any other type of direct mail. However, I received many irate owners calling or writing back asking me if I was plumb crazy because their

park was worth much more than I offered. On the flip side, I had several owners sign the contract and send it back. I purchased about 5 parks using this strategy.

How to Value an RV Park:

The "*market value*" on a typical appraisal report is defined as the:

"The most probable price which a property should bring in a competitive and open market under all conditions requisite to a fair sale, the buyer and seller each acting prudently, knowledgeably and assuming the price is not affected by undue stimulus. Implicit in this definition is the consummation of a sale as of a specified date and the passing of title from seller to buyer under conditions whereby:

1. Buyer and seller are typically motivated;

2. Both parties are well informed or well advised, and acting in what they consider their own best interests;

3. A reasonable time is allowed for exposure in the open market;

4. Payment is made in terms of cash in U.S. dollars or in terms of financial arrangements comparable thereto; and

5. The price represents a normal consideration for the property sold unaffected by special or creative financing or sale concessions granted by anyone associated with the sale."

Like most real estate the Seller usually wants "x+" and the purchaser wants to pay "x-" for an RV Park. The key is to get to negotiate to "x". Certain buyers may have different motivations for buying a certain park (1031 money, ability to obtain better financing, conversions to other uses, and location to where they want to live). In this book we only look at the value of an RV Park for the typical buyer who will continue to operate it as an RV Park.

The "Asking Price" is what the seller wants.

The "Selling Price" is what the seller gets.

Anyone that has seen an appraisal on a house or most types of real estate will have heard mention of the 3 approaches to determining the value of that real estate. They are the Cost, Sales, and Income Approach.

Cost Approach:

The Cost Approach is based on the reasoning that the park is worth what it would cost to find a comparable piece of land and build the improvements and then subtracting out a reasonable amount for depreciation. The problem with this method is that the business component and goodwill are not taken into account. The park may have been operated for many years and has built a substantial amount of repeat clientele and advertising presence. This "business aspect" is not addressed under the cost method. Unless you are coming up with the value of a brand new RV Park or one that was built in the last few years, then the cost method should only be used as a point of reference.

Sales Comparison Approach:

As far as the Sales or Market Comparison Approach to value, this is also highly suspect. This is based on comparing the sale of the subject property with other recent sales and adjusting for differences that you may or may not know about. Problems with this approach include varying expenses, rents, and management. Whether you are an investor or appraiser I would just use this approach as potential information and a point of reference. If you are looking for data on comparable sales you should contact Darrell Hess & Associates, who specialize in the marketing and sale of Campgrounds and RV Parks nationwide. They have a wealth of information which also includes industry data about the typical average income and expense ratios for seasonal and year round campground facilities.

Income Approach:

The third approach to value is the Income Approach and I find that this is really the best and only way to evaluate an RV Park correctly. I like to evaluate a park based on what it is currently doing, what it should be doing, and what it will do once I implement some basic changes and run it more efficiently.

Here is my standard process in estimating the value:

When evaluating an RV Park or Campground, I really want to know… What is in it for me? I don't really care about how much it cost to build the RV Park and all the amenities or what the park 500 miles down the road sold for. I want to know what I will get out of owning this park and if this is acceptable and it passes through my due diligence, then it is time to get out the checkbook (or credit cards if necessary)!

The most basic formulas are based on a gross income multiplier such as 3-5 times gross. So if a park is generating a gross income of $100,000 then the value is likely to be in the $300,000 to $500,000 range. This approach should only be used as a starting point to do a quick valuation. If the park is grossing $100,000 and the price is $1,000,000 then it may be either overpriced or have some other factors that must be researched in more detail. The same can hold true if the gross income is $100,000 and the park is priced at $200,000.

It might be underpriced, overpriced, or have some other factors that need to be evaluated.

The starting point in valuing an RV Park is to look at the Profit and Loss Statement that you receive from the seller or broker and then rework it to make it useful for you. Here are some of the important numbers that we will discuss:

Income - this is the income or sales that are generated from the RV Park. We only want to include the sources of income that will pass with the sale (don't include interest income on the parks bank account).

Cost of Goods Sold – this is the cost of the merchandise that was sold to customers (propane, gift shop items, parts and supplies).

Gross Profit - this is the income less the cost of goods sold.

Expenses - these are all the expenses you may find on the typical profit and loss statement.

Adjustments to Expenses to arrive at Operating Expenses - these are the amounts that we need to add to or subtract from the total Expenses to arrive at the Operating Expenses. We will remove the following types of expenses as part of the adjustment process:

- Depreciation and Amortization
- Mortgage interest
- Other interest
- Personal expenses such as:
- Travel & Entertainment not necessary for business operations
- Auto Expenses not necessary for the business

- Other items consumed by owner (groceries, gift shop items, etc)

- In addition, we will add to the expenses a reasonable amount (usually 2-5 percent) of the gross income as a reserve for replacements. While some years, there may be no capital improvements, there will be years when major improvements will need to be made. It is good to budget for these expenses every year so that when the time comes you will have the capital to do the improvements.

- To recap, we are taking the depreciation out and adding in the reserves for replacements number. The depreciation is based on the Income Tax laws and due to accelerated depreciation methods, it will typically be a higher number than the actual amount needed each year to replace or upgrade the park infrastructure and equipment.

Also, we will adjust the expenses to either include a management expense (if there is none listed) or adjust the amount that is listed as the owner's salary or management expense. You will often find that there is no management expense at all if the current owner is running the property. Other times, you will find a line item titled "owner's salary" and this may be high or low. If you are going to be running the park you deserve a fair amount of compensation for that time and effort. This amount should be comparable to what it would cost to have someone do the work for you such as an onsite manager or property management firm. In order to get the true picture and arrive at a more accurate net operating income, and net owner benefit, you need to replace this amount with a reasonable amount. You can check wages for other hospitality type properties and make necessary adjustments. The management expense is typically in the 5-10 percent of gross range.

Operating Expenses - these are the expenses necessary to operate the business. We arrive at this number by taking the total Expenses above and applying the adjustments we just made to that number.

Net Operating Income - this is the amount that the business should generate in spendable cash to pay debt service as well as put in the pocket of the owner.

Net Owner's Benefit - this is an amount that can be calculated by taking the Net Operating Income and adding to it any extra benefits the owner will receive. These additions typically include housing and utilities. Find out the typical rent for similar housing and utilities in the area and then add this to the Net Operating Income to come up with the Net Owner's Benefit.

Here is a list of the most common types of expenses. Not every park has all of these expenses and some have additional expenses but this is a good starting point.

- Advertising (mail, directories, promotions, signs, billboards, yellow pages, other)
- Amortization (goodwill)
- Auto Expense (may be park related but many times has personal auto expenses)
- Bank Service Charges (Bank account and Credit Card Processing)
- Depreciation (a non cash expense)
- Franchise Fees (KOA's)
- Insurance: Liability (could include personal autos)
- Insurance: Property

- Insurance: Workers Comp (if you have employees you need workers comp)

- Insurance: Medical & Life (If on the owners, then is a personal expense)

- Interest: Mortgage and Other

- Legal and Accounting (may include one-time fees or personal issues)

- Licenses and Permits

- Maintenance Labor

- Management Offsite

- Management Onsite

- Mowing & Landscaping

- Payroll: Manager, Maintenance

- Postage (could include many personal letters)

- Rent Discounts & Incentives (Travel Clubs & Membership Discounts)

- Repairs: Equipment

- Repairs: Pool

- Repairs: Road

- Repairs: Utilities

- Repairs: Other

- Reserve for Capital Improvements (usually not on the owner's P & L)

- Supplies: Maintenance

- Supplies: Office (could include school supplies, software games, etc)
- Taxes: Payroll
- Taxes: Property
- Telephone (is there a separate phone for the owner's personal use)
- Travel (usually personal)
- Utilities: Cable
- Utilities: Electric
- Utilities: Gas
- Utilities: Trash
- Utilities: Water & Sewer
- Utilities: Wi-fi
- Web Site
- Workers Compensation

Not all of these will be applicable for every RV Park, but it wouldn't hurt to go through these one by one and see if they are included or not. If you believe the RV Park should have certain expenses that are in this list and not on any of the statements then you should ask the seller. Many expenses such as insurance, taxes, and utilities can be verified with the agency or company providing the services.

Reworking the Profit and Loss Statement: Here is the process to rework the Profit and Lost Statement:

1. First we will subtract out the interest income earned from the businesses checking account to get to the appropriate Income number.

2. Next we will make sure that the cost of any of the products sold to our guests are listed in the Cost of Goods Sold Section (if the RV Park has a significant amount of sales from these products then you should enlist the services of a professional to help you dissect this information).

3. Next we will look at all of the other expenses listed and make adjustments to this total by adding or subtracting the following types of expenses.

    • Depreciation and Amortization

    • Adjust Salaries and Management Expenses

    • Non Recurring Expenses

    • Personal Expenses

    • Repair & Maintenance expenses that should have been capitalized

    • Interest Expenses

    • Reserve for Replacements

This will give us the Operating Expenses figure.

4. Next we will take the Gross Profit and subtract the Operating Expenses from that to arrive at the Net Operating Income.

5. From the Net Operating Income we add the following types of expenses/benefits that the owner will receive to arrive at the Net Owner's Benefit.

    • Rental value of onsite living quarters (may be an upstairs apartment above the office, a site built home, or mobile home)

- Utilities paid by the park for the owner's consumption – water, sewer, trash, gas, electric, cable, wi-fi and the list goes on.

- The amount of money earmarked for the management and maintenance services that the owner will complete which was inserted into the operating expenses.

- This will leave you with a number that is referred to as the Net Owner's benefit. Based on the seller's numbers and your reworking of the profit and loss statement, this is the amount of cash and other benefits you will receive from owning the RV Park. Note: there are also other benefits that you should receive as the owner which will include income tax advantages through the use of depreciation, build up of equity as the mortgage is paid down, and hopefully appreciation of the property as you continue to increase the Net Operating Income for many years to come.

Ok, so I know what the net operating income and net owner benefit is, what should I pay for the park?

This question can have many different answers based on several different factors. The value an RV Park may be $2 million for one person and $1.5 million to someone else. The key is really deciding what you are willing to pay based on your expectations of what type of return you want on your investment. This return on investment will come in several different forms:

- Monthly/Yearly Cash Flow

- Tax Savings

- Equity Buildup

- Appreciation

- Rent Increases and Expense Reductions
- Other Benefits

In addition to these returns on investment, the value of a park can depend on the financing terms offered by the seller or the availability of financing from other sources. Other factors may include the area of the country you want to live, type of RV Park (overnight, seasonal, etc), whether you want a year round operation or a seasonal one.

In deciding what you should pay for the park, I will show you two different approaches. By going through both approaches you should be able to arrive at a figure that the Park is worth to you as the buyer. The first approach is to use the Net Operating Income figure and apply a capitalization rate to it. The other approach is to figure out what you want out of the property in terms of cash and other benefits and use the Net Owner Benefit figure.

Net Operating Income and Capitalization Rate Approach: The Net Operating Income is the amount left over to pay the debt service and go into the owner's pocket. This is also the number that is used to arrive at a value if you were using a capitalization rate approach (cap rate). The cap rate is the amount you should earn on your investment supposing that you paid all cash for it. You will want a higher cap rate as the risk increases (if you can earn a rate of return of 5 percent on a CD which is virtually risk free, you will want to earn a higher rate of return on other investments as this risk increases).

Take the Net Operating Income and divide by the appropriate cap rate to arrive at the value. Cap rates for RV Parks and Campgrounds are all over the board. I have seen parks sell for as little as a 5% cap rate up to well over 15%. In recent years due to rapid appreciation of properties in many areas, investors have been buying at low Cap Rates to speculate on this appreciation. However, on average parks are listed for sale at a cap rate in the range of 8-13% with a final sales price more in the 11% range. Where a particular property falls within these averages will depend on many factors.

Also, it is important to note that cap rates tend to increase when interest rates go up and decrease when interest rates decline. If you think about this, it makes sense due to the fact that at lower interest rates you pay less of a monthly loan payment and have more cash to spend. Sellers want in on this windfall and they and the market tends to push the prices up when interest rates are lower.

What is a good cap rate? The answer is really up to the buyer. Some buyers tell me they want at least a 7 cap, some say 10 cap, some say 20 cap (I say good luck to these people).

So in reality, a certain RV Park will have a different value to each and every person. The idea is to decide what you want or will require in terms of your investment and then work to make the deal fit these requirements.

If you want a 10 cap on a property priced at a 7 cap, it does not necessarily mean you should pass on the deal. For instance, the park may be mismanaged or is not open as long as it should be. By making a few simple changes you may be able to increase the income very quickly and have the 10 cap you want. If the rents are under market or there are expenses that can be reduced or other ways to increase the net income with minimal work and cash outlay you might pay extra for a park if it otherwise meets your investment criteria.

As my general rule when dealing with parks that are borderline but have the potential to increase in value and offer an acceptable return on investment by increasing income or reducing expense: I generally will add up to 50% of the value from these quick fixes to my offer on a park. So if I can increase the income and reduce expenses and this increases the value of the park by $100,000, then I would consider adding $50,000 to my offer price if necessary. After all, we should earn something from our expertise and doing what the owner could have done already.

Net Owners Benefit Approach to Value: This approach addresses what you want out of a park more in terms of the cash flow and other benefits to see if it makes sense.

The starting point is to decide how much of a down payment you have for an RV Park and then multiply that down payment by 4. This should give you an approximate price range of what you can afford. So, if you have $250,000 for a down payment, you should be able to buy a one million dollar park.

The next step is to decide how much money you will need for that $250,000 investment to generate so that you can earn the type of living you are comfortable with. Suppose you want that investment to provide your housing, utilities, and an additional $50,000 per year. Now that you know what your requirements are, you will start looking for RV Parks that will produce these results or better in areas that you are comfortable with.

Take an RV Park with a net operating income of $100,000 and a price tag of $1,000,000. If you were able to buy this with seller or bank financing with 25 percent down with an interest rate of 8 percent and amortized over 25 years, you would have an approximate monthly payment of $5,800.00 and a yearly payment of $60,000.00. Subtract the $60,000 from the net operating income and you have $40,000 left over. Next assume that in the expenses, to come up with the Net Operating Income, you budgeted $10,000 to pay yourself. So you would receive the $40,000 plus the $10,000 for a total of $50,000. If you receive your housing and other benefits that you desire, this park seems like it would fit. Of course, there may be other issues to address such as deferred maintenance that may require initial capital right away. You will find these in due diligence and can either renegotiate or pass on the deal and look elsewhere. On the other hand, you may find areas that you know you can improve on right away and increase the net income by $10,000 per year from the start. All purchases and properties are different and one or more of these factors will come into play on most of them. You should always have a comfort level and some additional capital in case a problem arises.

A note about the terms: Changing the interest rate to 9% would increase the payment by $5,000 per year and make this deal less appealing. On the flip side a decrease in the interest rate by 1 percent would decrease the payment by over $5,000 per year and make it even more attractive. Also reducing or lengthening the term of the loan will also increase or decrease the payment. Here are a couple of strategies that have worked well for me when negotiating on seller financing:

1.   Offer a lower interest rate for the first couple of years in order to increase your cash flow and comfort level. If a seller wants an 8% interest rate and is willing to carry long term, it may not kill the deal if you offer 6% for years 1 and 2 and then 7% for years 3 and 4 and then go to 8% for years 5-7. You could even go up to say 10% for years 8-25. At that time depending on whether it would be favorable or not, you can refinance, put money in your pocket and lower your payments with a new loan.

2. Stagger your down payment. If the seller wants $250,000.00 down payment, you could offer to give him a down payment of $150,000.00 now, put $50,000.00 into improving the park, and then give him an extra $25,000 at the end of year one and year two. You would still be putting out the $250,000.00 but $50,000.00 of it goes directly into increasing the value or the park (which gives the seller more security) and $50,000.00 is spread out over a couple of years.

3. possibility that works well when the seller has a loan to payoff or needs a larger down payment is to obtain a bank loan for say 60% of the value of the park and then have the seller carry back as a second mortgage 20-25%. In this case the seller would receive 75 to 80 percent of the purchase price.

Another Variation to Valuation: another way I like to break down the valuation of an RV Park or Campground is to take each significant portion of the business and value each portion as if it were its own business. This would only be necessary and logical in the case of an RV Park that has significant other income streams (such as convenience stores, gas pumps, propane sales, bars, restaurants, boat rentals, guide services, etc). If you are able to break each income item down with its corresponding expenses then you will not only see how each area of the business is doing but also have the opportunity to evaluate whether some of the profit centers are worth the extra effort. However, be careful when cutting things out as one part of the business that is operating at a loss or breakeven may be fueling other more lucrative parts of the business.

After you have broken these separate areas of the business out, you might give them a different valuation. For example, a net profit of $10,000 on seasonal RV's or mobile home monthly rentals is going to take a lot less effort than overnight RV's. Also, serving food, running an arcade, or selling propane is more time intensive than renting out an overnight lot.

To simplify this example, I might pay a 10 percent cap for the seasonal RV's and monthly mobile homes, a 12 cap for overnight RV's, and a 14 cap for the restaurant and store sales.

Other Value Considerations: If you have been looking at RV Parks to buy for some time, you will have likely heard something that goes like this: "this is a cash business and a lot of income does not hit the books". In addition, you will hear: "I write off everything through the park…groceries, cell phones, new cars, gas, and the list goes on".

The goal of the owner/accountant is to prepare the financial records to minimize profits and reduce the overall income tax liability. While this is a good goal to have, it is best to do so legally. This approach is opposite of the goal of public corporations who want to show strong profits in order to look good to their shareholders and Wall Street.

When the owner does not report income or claims bogus expenses, they are on one hand defrauding the government and on the other trying to tell you to believe them that their park is really more profitable in reality than on paper. While they may be telling you the truth, it is double standards… pay fewer taxes and sell for more money. Unless you work for the IRS you are not going to want to worry about whether they can or should deduct everything they are currently deducting and you already know it is illegal to not report income. What you want to know is whether the park is producing the net income that is shown on the books and tax returns or is the net income really this amount plus $50,000.? Unless the owner has a second set of books with a paper trail that he can show you entailing the true picture, you will either have to take his word or find some other way of verifying what is going on.

One thing is certain even if the owner can convince you that there is more income than is reported is…it will be difficult to convince your banker that this is the case. You have a strong position to negotiate for owner financing if they really want to sell.

As far as verifying the expenses that are being run through the park on the tax returns you should be able to go through these with the seller on a one to one basis and see receipts, checks, or other verification. The problem here is that the seller may be paying cash for some of the expenses and not getting receipts. So even though there may be more income than is reported, there may be increased expenses as well.

In evaluating the fact that the income is not all going through the books, this is usually more difficult to get a handle on. One way to look into this would be to go back through the registrations (check in sheets) and see if they add up to more than is being claimed. Another way would be to take a close look at the utility expenses and find out the average amount of electricity or water that is used by a typical RVer and then back into an estimate of how many RVers were staying there in a given month. There are a lot of factors to take into account with this approach and unless you are very good analytically, I would consider hiring an expert.

Another approach which may work is to include as part of your due diligence period something called an "Observation Period". An observation period is that period after a property is under contract in which the purchaser is allowed to observe the day-to-day business operation first hand. As long as the park is in season, this will allow you to see what the actual income flow is. In addition, this would be a great way to become acquainted with the particular business. Getting the seller to agree to this observation period will likely allow you to see the true picture. If the seller will not allow this observation period, then I would strongly consider that the seller may be hiding something. Even if the seller is keeping good records and you are not concerned with the true picture of the park, you will learn a great deal about the RV Park business and particularly about the RV Park you are considering purchasing. When you read through the due diligence portion of this book, think about how many of these items could be confirmed or reconfirmed during a one or two week observation period.

In addition to this "observation period" if you feel it would be beneficial to have the seller stay on for a month or two to teach/train you on the business, you might consider inserting into your contract something to that effect that the seller agrees to stay on for a certain time period to work with and train the new buyer. This is usually a plus because they can help you learn the business even if you learn how badly they are running the business.

Energetic Owners and those with Specialized Knowledge: Sometimes you will find those owners/managers that are truly one-of-a-kind. They have this extra sense of energy, enthusiasm, and have built a great RV Business. With their personality and knowledge they may have people staying there just to be a part of this enthusiasm or benefit in some way from their knowledge. In addition to this type of owner, consider an owner that has a park in which he also runs a guide service (fishing or hunting) and he knows where all the best spots are and is bringing this extra knowledge to the business. If you are going to be buying a park from sellers that have a situation as this, you will want to continue providing this excellent service. You may not be able to improve on this type of park right away, but if you obtain as much one-on-one time with the seller, you may be able to learn and get up to speed quickly.

Of course, this can be just the opposite when you are buying a park where the owner/manager would rather watch television or play on the internet than take care of the business and guests. You should be able to turn this place around if everything else checks out.

In most cases when you review a sales package for an RV Park for sale it will not mention any reserve for capital expenditures. This really should be addressed in your evaluation of the park and in the due diligence phase. Items like replacing all the water lines or sewer lines for older parks, resurfacing the roads, topping all the trees, are large expenses that can occur in the future and should be budgeted for. While they are not expensed for income tax purposes they are capitalized and depreciated over 15 years or so, and are therefore real costs. I would include at least 2-5% of gross income as a Reserve for Capital Improvements in your numbers when determining the value.

You will find some sellers that expense everything and then find the opposite where owners capitalize as much as possible to make the bottom line look better. Spend some time going through all the expenses and estimating future capital improvements.

Other considerations on the value of the park will be the entrances, streets, landscaping, utilities, parking, lights, storage sheds, number of singles versus doubles, swimming pools, clubhouses, etc. The nicer the park typically the lower the cap rate and the easier it will be to tap into better financing programs.

Comprehensive Example

Pertinent Facts:

- Price of $800,000.00

- New Mortgage with 25% down, $600,000 new loan at 8.00% interest and amortized over 30 years).

- 100 Spaces on 15 acres

- Seller currently lives in the park and takes care of all management & maintenance.

Adjustments & Assumptions:

We are assuming the income numbers reported are correct. We will verify them more in due diligence.

- *Interest Income* – this amount is from the seller's business bank account and unfortunately he will not be transferring the money in the account to us at closing so we need to remove this line item: Deduct $2,000

- *Advertising Expense:* Current owner does not run any advertising and at a minimum we will spend $500 per month to run various ad campaigns to increase occupancy: Add $6,000

- *Amortization Expense:* This is goodwill that the seller is amortizing from when he purchased the property. Non Cash Expense: Deduct $500.00

- *Auto Expense:* The seller is writing off the gas and repairs on a work truck he uses in the park and also his Corvette. We estimate that about half of this expense is going for the personal use of the Corvette. Deduct $3,000.00.

- *Depreciation Expense:* This is a non cash expense as well as an expense for income tax purposes and so we will remove it. Deduct $30,000. Note on Depreciation: If we purchase the park, we will most likely have a larger tax basis for depreciation and will have a larger depreciation expense.

- **Insurance Expense:** Seller has had the same insurance with low limits and insufficient coverage's for several years – a new quote was received at $3,000 per year with 1 million coverage and standard community insurance. Add $2,000

- **Management:** We estimate that the new owner (husband and wife) will work a total of 60 hours per week on average for 6 months (26 weeks). After researching the local area we have found that the going rate for management of hospitality type properties is $8 per hour plus lodging and utilities. 60 x 8 x 26 = $12,480. Add $12,480.

- **Work Campers:** To keep our sanity, we will hire two work campers and offer them free space rent and utilities for the season. In return for this, they will fill in for us in the office one or two days per week and be available to help with maintenance for a couple of hours per week. We will also pay payroll taxes ($500.00) obtain a workers comp insurance policy ($500.00) for them. Payroll: Taxes add $500 and Payroll: Workers Comp add $500.

- **Repairs & Maintenance:** It appears that the repairs and maintenance expense is very low. This may be due to the fact the owner is very thrifty and does all the work himself or that he forgot to add in some expenses to this statement. We find out that he is thrifty and handy. In fact, he does all the plumbing and electrical work himself. We know how to plug things in and flush the toilet but that is the extent of it. We will hire local contractors for this work and estimate it to be $4,000 per year. Add $4,000 to Repairs and Maintenance.

- **Repairs & Maintenance:** Also the owner has a grader that has been in the family since 1952. He has been grading the roads 3 times per year. He is going to take it with him and so we are going to have to hire a company to do this for us. Add an estimated $2,000 per year to Repairs and Maintenance.

- **Reserve for Replacements:** After looking at the current infrastructure (roads, utilities, buildings), we determine that they appear to be maintained well. However, we know that we will have to make upgrades and major repairs from time to time. We estimate that we will spend approximately $6,000 per year for capital improvements. Add $6,000 to Reserve for Replacements.

   Property taxes are based on 1.5% of the assessed value and the assessed value is currently $400,000. We estimate the assessed value will go up after the sale to $800,000. Add $6,000 to Taxes: Property.

- **Travel & Entertainment.** The owner has been taking a cross country trip every year driving around and looking at other RV Parks (to see how they are running their business and get ideas). However, he spends most of this time visiting National Parks and Fishing. We are not going to travel cross country and write it off as a business expense. Add $3,000 to Travel & Entertainment.

After determining the Net Operating Income we can make some adjustments to this amount to calculate the Net Owner Benefit. With this RV Park, there is 2,000 square foot site built home that will serve as the owner's quarters. The market rent in the area for a similar type of house is $750 per month. In addition, the RV Park has been paying the utilities for this house and based on other housing in the area we have concluded that this equates to $250 per month. Also, note that we included a line item above for the Management Expense to be reserved for the new owner. This was $12,480 per year.

- Adjustments: Housing: Add $9,000
- Utilities: Add $3,000
- Management: Add $12,480

This will give us the Net Owner Benefit amount.

Cap Rate: We can determine the cap rate now that we have the Net Operating Income and Price. Cap Rate = Net Operating Income divided by Price. In this case the cap rate is calculated and we have come up with 10 percent.

Cash on Cash Return: This is the return you will receive on your down payment. To calculate this, you take the Net Operating Income less the Yearly Loan Payments and divide this amount by your down payment.

Yearly Cash Flow: In addition, we can determine the anticipated yearly cash flow. We take the Net Operating Income and subtract out the Yearly Loan Payments and add to this the amount of Management Expense. This is the amount the Owner will have to spend each year from the business. As the income increases and the expenses decrease this should go up.

The rest of the expenses are listed below in the Profit & Loss Calculations:

> **Note:** When you receive the profit and loss statement you should also request a copy of the income tax statements as well. When you put the numbers side by side from these statements you will get a better picture of the true operations. The income on the profit and loss is usually either the same or higher than that reported on the tax return. In addition, the expenses on the tax return are usually the same or higher than those on

the profit and loss statement. There may also be cases when some income items and expense items are overstated, understated or missing on both statements. Record keeping is not always a high priority and receipts go missing and some things are forgotten. In this example, we are assuming that the tax return and profit and loss statement are in agreement.

For most of these items that are in question, you should be able to get statements from the company providing the service as well as receipts, bank statements, and canceled checks from the seller.

Income	P & L - Owner	Adjustments	Adjusted P & L
Registration Income	$170,000	$0	$170,000
Store Sales	20,000	0	20,000
Propane Sales	10,000	0	10,000
Vending/Games	5,000	0	5,000
Interest Income	2,000	-2,000	0
Total Income			**$205,000**
Cost of Goods Sold			
Store	$15,000	$0	$15,000
Propane	7,000	0	7,000
Vending/Games	3,000	0	3,000
Additional Services	3,000	0	3,000
Total of Cost of Goods Sold			**$28,000**
Gross Profit			$177,000
Operating Expenses			
Advertising	$0	$6,000	$6,000
Amortization Expense	500	-500	0
Auto Expense	6,000	-3,000	3,000
Bank & Credit Card Charges	2,500	0	2,500
Depreciation Expense	25,000	-25,000	0
Insurance	1,000	2,000	3,000
Interest Expense - Mortgage	30,000	-30,000	0
Interest Expense - Other	3,000	-3,000	0
Legal & Accounting	1,000	0	1,000
Licenses & Permits	500	0	500
Maintenance Supplies	1,000	0	1,000
Management Expense	0	12,480	12,480
Office Supplies	1,000	0	1,000
Payroll: Taxes	0	500	500
Payroll: Workers Comp	0	500	500
Promotion: Website	500	0	500
Repairs & Maintenance	2,500	6,000	8,500

Income	P & L - Owner	Adjustments	Adjusted P & L
Reserve for Replacements	0	6,000	6,000
Taxes: Property	6,000	6,000	12,000
Taxes: Sales	8,000	0	8,000
Travel & Entertainment	3,000	-3,000	0
Travel Club Discounts/Royalties	2,000	0	2,000
Utilities: Cable TV	3,000	0	3,000
Utilities: Gas and Electric	15,000	0	15,000
Utilities: Telephone	1,500	0	1,500
Utilities: Trash	4,000	0	4,000
Utilities: Water and Sewer	5,000	0	5,000
Total Operating Expenses			**$96,980**
Net Operating Income			$80,020
Other Considerations:			
Owner Housing			$9,000
Owner Utilities			3,000
Management(paid to owner)			12,480
Total Other Considerations:			$24,480
Total Owner Benefit			$104,500
Purchase Price			$800,000
Cap Rate			10.00%
Yearly Loan Payments			$52,831
Cash on Cash Return			13.59%
Yearly Cash Flow			$39,669

Is this RV Park a good deal? It all depends on what you want as a return on your investment. If you are looking strictly in terms of cap rate and you want a 10.00% cap rate or higher, then it should be a good fit. If you are looking at cash on cash returns and are able to get the proposed financing as shown and a return of 13.59 percent is acceptable then it is good on this front as well. Additional considerations can be given to return on equity, income tax savings, and other investment formulas.

Owner Benefit Scenario

If you look at this based on the benefits you will get as the owner and they are within the goals you have set then it should work as well. In this case you should be receiving $39,669 per year in cash benefits plus free lodging and utilities. Besides these apparent benefits, you will also be living at your business (no commuting costs or headaches), you will have 6 months off per year to do whatever it is you want, and your property should appreciate in value and your equity will increase from this as well as from the principle reductions you make on your loan.

It all goes back to the Willing Buyer scenario we discussed earlier. If this is what you are looking for and you are a Willing Buyer, then go for it! But only after you complete your due diligence! This is the next topic.

Due Diligence:

When you put an RV Park under contract you will definitely want to have a stipulation in the contract that will allow you confirm what the seller has said so far as well as evaluate the overall feasibility of the purchase. Due Diligence will look at the physical, economic, demographic and market feasibility of the project. This time period is usually between 30 and 60 days.

In conducting your due diligence you are looking to identify anything that poses a potential issue and that **you are able to change or fix.** These usually deal with the cleanliness of the park (junk & trash piled up), mismanagement, lack of rule enforcement, collections, expenses that can be reduced.

But more importantly you are looking for those problems that you **may not be able to fix or that will be very expensive to fix.** These types of issues usually deal with the size of the lots, reputation, problems with location, flood plains, drainage problems, bad configuration of lots, water, sewer, electric, and gas line problems.

In conducting your due diligence you may call on experts in surveying, accounting, marketing, financing, plumbing, electrical, and legal.

Ask the Seller to provide you with the following (if applicable):

1. City, County and State Permits and Licenses

2. Sewer Plant Records and Readings

3. Water Well Tests and Compliance Records

4. Existing Surveys or Environmental Reports

5. Water and other Utility Meter Reading Records and Formulas

6. Property tax bills for the last 2-3 years

7. List of all Personal Property (Equipment) that is to be transferred at closing

8. Copy of current insurance policy and binder showing premiums and coverage's

9. Current staffing list including position, wages, job descriptionsAny drawings and maps of the park and infrastructure and size of lots

10. Any Contracts that will be transferred to buyer at closing (laundry, trash, phone)

11. Affiliations with Camping & RV clubs and Franchise Agreements.

12. Current advertising agreements with National RV directories (Woodall's, Good Sam's, etc)

13. Bank Statements

14. 2-3 years Tax Returns

15. 2-3 years Profit and Loss

16. List of Capital Expenditures for the last 3 years

17. Listing of any current park infrastructure problems (water, sewer, gas, electric)

18. Any prior or potential future jumps in occupancy due to major construction projects

19. List of all reservations for upcoming year

20. For parks with permanent occupants: Rent Roll with specific homesite number, name of resident, move-in date, monthly rent, current balance, additional charges, number of occupants, and a brief history of the resident (good resident / bad resident, special circumstances, etc)

21. Names and phone numbers of all of all contractors used in the last few years – plumbers, electricians, propane, gas, roto rooters

As you are receiving this information from the Seller you will want to evaluate it with the other information you receive from outside sources.

If you do not take anything else from this book make sure you read this section very carefully.

Here is a quote I that I have slowly learned to live by and is the driving force behind my due diligence process.

"Your Instincts STINK…Do Proper Due Diligence"

Doing proper due diligence will save you from making potentially hundreds of thousands of dollars in mistakes. In addition, it will allow you to learn about the park you are looking to purchase and if you find something that is needing attention, you will have the facts and figures to either scrap the deal or renegotiate to make the deal work.

I have heard the saying many times that "you make your money when you buy the property". I would like to add something to this and that is "you will potentially lose more money by not doing your due diligence than you will ever make". Many times properties that are priced so well that they are too good to be true are exactly that... too good to be true.

Here is a list of the items you should consider in doing your Due Diligence.

These are not necessarily in any order:

1. ***Park Location Issues:*** You cannot change the location so this is very important: If the park is an overnight type park where people stop to rest for the night, then a park with good highway or exit ramp visibility or good signage directing RVer's to the park is important. Being in close proximity to other services such as restaurants and gas stations is helpful. If the park is a destination park, then being in close proximity to the National park or other attraction is important. Travelers will typically prefer to stay near the attractions they are there to visit. If the park is a seasonal park which attracts residents for months at a time, then being nearby to shopping, restaurants, hospitals, and other services is more desirable and can generate higher rents compared to the parks out in the sticks. When you visit a park that you are considering purchasing and you get lost finding it, then you should consider that potential RVer's are also going to have the same problem.

2. ***Flood Plain:*** Is the park located in a flood plain? If so, when was the last time it flooded? If the park does flood, are their any restrictions against allowing monthly or more permanent residency? Will the homeowners be required to have flood

insurance? Flood plain issues are typically not as important for RV Parks as they are for Mobile Home Parks. However, they may still be deal killers under some circumstances. In many cases, Mobile Home Parks that are in flood plain are being converted to RV Parks as it is much easier to move an RV to higher ground in the case flooding. Here is an example of a park that I was looking at purchasing that demonstrates this point.

About 10 years ago I was looking at some mobile home parks in the Dallas, Texas area. In looking at these parks I found a park that had about 100 spaces and the numbers were great. However, while I was driving through the park I noticed that many of the lots were occupied with RV's rather than mobile homes. This was a very good market and the lots were big enough to hold mobile homes so I wondered why so many lots had RV's rather than mobile homes. After talking with the owner, it came up that the park was in a flood zone and the city was not allowing any more mobile homes to move in the park. The problem was that the park kept flooding every couple of years and each time it flooded, more mobile homes were being destroyed and being pulled out. Since the owner could not rent these vacant lots to mobiles, she had to rent to RV's. Luckily for her, the market was such that there was a strong demand for RV's to rent by the month and it kept the income coming in.

Don't always take the seller's word about whether the park is in a flood plain or not. I did this once only to find out about a month after the purchase that the park flooded badly and was prone to flooding every few years. You can talk to surrounding property owners to find out about flooding issues. In addition, you should be able to receive a copy of the FEMA flood map on the property which will show the property and any parts of it that are in a flood plain.

3. ***100 year and 500 year Flood Plains: In most cases,*** buying a park in a 100 year or 500 year flood zone will not come back to bite you. However, you should definitely understand the risks involved. Most of the time your renters will just have to carry flood insurance and your lender will require the same for your buildings and utility connections.

4. ***Noise Problems:*** Loud outside noise can often be a deterrent for living in a certain RV Park. Being located close to highways or busy streets without sound barriers and also nearby trains can be very annoying to potential residents.

    I owned a Mobile Home & RV Park near Victoria, Texas and I was in the manager's home one time and here comes a train. The whole trailer shook and you could not even carry on a conversation until it had passed by. It was definitely a nuisance and I guess it happened there about 10 times per day. I realized why it had been so hard to rent any of the Monthly RV spaces that were nearest to the train tracks. The mobile home section stayed full as the market was good. However I had a hard time renting any of the RV sites because of the train noise.

5. ***Required Licenses: Find out if the*** park is required to be licensed and if so that it has the required license. You will want to check that the park is operating in compliance with the license. If a park has 50 units but is licensed for only 25, you may have potential problems. The license may be issued by the State, County, or Local authorities. Often it is issued with the State Board of Health.

6. ***Other Profit Center Licenses:*** Also, if the park is operating other profit centers that require a specific license, you want to make sure that these are transferable or easily attainable. You may need a license to run a restaurant, bar, store with beer sales, guide service in national forests, etc. You want to make sure you have these licenses in place as soon as possible so you do not have to close down parts of the business while you wait for approval. I was once looking to broker an RV Park which had a bar out front that was also operated by the current owner. The income from the bar was significant but the park was in Texas and due to the laws at the time, a new owner had to have been a resident of Texas for a couple of years to get the liquor license. So it narrowed down the potential buyers significantly.

7. ***Long Term Issues:*** If you are looking at an RV park that is renting spaces on a longer term basis (monthly or yearly), or if you plan on converting some of the spaces to a longer term, then you will also need to check with the State, County, Local restrictions that may limit the amount of time an RV is allowed to be parked there. In many cases, this can be 30 days, 3 months, or 6 months.

8. ***Grandfathered Zoning:*** Some cities have laws that state that if a certain percentage of the homes in a park that has "grandfathered" zoning are destroyed, then those lots will not be allowed to be rented again. This can happen from fire, tornado, hurricane, etc. This is usually more important to check into when you have mobile home sites or long term RV sites. Always, check the local codes.

9. ***Review Reports:*** Review any park inspection reports conducted by the State Board of Health or other City/County

inspectors. In some states, especially those where licenses are required, the state does an annual inspection and produces a report with notices of any violations. It is good to see these violations and be sure that they have been corrected.

10. *Directory Rating:* In addition, to the state and county inspections it would also be a good idea to see how the park is rated in the Trailer Life, Woodalls, and other Campground rating directories. Many of the RVer's out there consult these directories and base their travel plans on the ratings, amenities, etc that are in these directories. If the park is not in the directory, this is a must if you wish to increase the occupancy.

11. *Management Expectations:* If you will not be operating the park yourself and are considering hiring the current management you may want to have friends or associates make a few calls to the property and see how the management handles the calls. Also, if you visit the manager's home and it is not kept up good and they have a set of rules for themselves rather than abiding with the general park rules, it may be an indication that you should look for other management.

12. *Interview the Customers:* After you have the park under contract and usually after you have the owner's permission it is definitely a good idea to interview some of the current and past park campers/residents. They are usually full of information when it comes to finding out how the park is actually operating. You will often hear about water problems, sewer problems, and any other common problems by talking to the residents.

13. *Talk to RV Dealers:* Another good source of information would be the local recreational vehicle dealers. They usually

know about most of the parks and can give you information on the parks reputation, whether they have in the past and will in the future refer the park to potential residents, etc.

14. **Visit the Park:** If possible, you will want to visit the park at various times of the day, morning, noon, after dark as you will be able to see the park as it is. It is also advisable to see the park during the week and on the weekends. This will give you a better indication of parking, occupancy, lighting, as well as noise level. You might also ask to be in the office during the busy times of the day so that you can get a feel for what questions are asked by campers and see the actual operating procedures (check-in, check-out, payment, etc) currently in effect. If you are new to buying RV parks, this will really get you acquainted with the business.

15. **Chamber of Commerce:** The local Chamber of Commerce is also a wealth of information. They can give you information on population trends, travel and traffic numbers, area attractions, other tourism members and data, new and current employers, potential plant shutdowns, as well as the general market conditions of an area.

16. **Real Estate Brokers:** Local Real Estate Brokers can also provide information on the area and market and real estate outlooks. This may include such things as hot areas of the city, where the building is going on, and other pertinent facts.

17. **Tax Assessors:** Contact the Property Tax Office: to check tax rates and whether taxes are current. Learn what their assessment procedures are so that you can estimate how much you will be paying in taxes if you purchase the park.

18. ***Get the Numbers and Verify:*** Verify the deposits as well as copies of receipts to verify that the amount actually collected is being reflected correctly. Often times, park owners forget to tell you that they give some people discounts (seniors, friends, relatives, etc). Also, you will find out that many RV parks take cash payments that go straight in the owner's pocket and never show up in the bank account or tax returns. This can make getting bank financing much more difficult when the operating numbers do not match the tax returns.

    A case in point: I was looking at brokering a Mobile Home and RV Park several years ago. It was approximately half Mobile Home and half RV. Needless the say, the owners were in their retirement years with pictures of grandkids all over the place. During the discussions I was looking at the Profit & Loss Statements and noticed that there was no income from the RV portion of the park. They explained that they only took cash for the RV spaces and it went directly into their pockets. This park was in a very high tourist area and a simple calculation revealed this amounted to somewhere in the range of $75,000 per year. It is very difficult to explain this to potential buyers so I did not take the listing.

19. ***For Insurance Purposes:*** Make sure to verify the pet restrictions and leash laws as well as the enforcement of such. Most insurance carriers do not allow dangerous breeds of dogs or even dogs over 20 – 30 pounds. Also make sure that the swimming pool, propane filling stations, and other potential risk have the appropriate safety precautions.

20. ***Water Lines:*** what are they made of? Are there signs of water leaks? Is the water pressure acceptable? Many times you will have some areas of the park where the water pressure is much

lower than the rest. You can have water pressure tests done on different areas of the park as well as talk with current residents about the water pressure (after you have permission).

In addition, you should review bills from the utility companies from the same month over a couple years to locate any major problems/leaks. In addition, these utility bills will often reveal the occupancy levels as well. In a summer RV park the usage will be much more during the busy times of the year in comparison to the winter.

21. ***Sewer Lines:*** typically you will have problems with older sewer lines: clay pipe and thin walled plastic pipes. Clay pipes will allow large tree roots to start growing inside which will start causing backups. In addition clay & thin walled sewer pipes will also tend to crumble and then plug up. You may be able to have a camera check out the pipes as well as have them professionally blown out with high speed water jets as periodic maintenance.

I have run into this problem many times in the past. I purchase a park and then a few days or months later, I start getting many calls from the manager and then bills from Roto Rooters and Plumbers with the same conclusion. The sewer pipes are clay tiles and are plugged up from tree roots or just caved in. If you are purchasing a park that has these types of sewer lines, then you will definitely want to include the future costs of replacements in your negotiations.

22. ***Electric Service:*** You will want to check whether the electric is above ground or below ground. If above, you will generally be responsible for the main electric poles so take a look at

the electric poles to see if they are rotting near ground level. These can be quite expensive to replace.

Another potential electric issue is that most of the newer RV's need 30 or 50 amp service. Many of the older parks have not been upgraded to this level of service and will need to be in the future to stay competitive. This will usually require an upgrade which will usually cost $300-$800 in parts and labor to upgrade a single meter.

23. **Gas Service:** If you are responsible for the gas meters and lines then you may want to have the system pressure tested as a small gas leak can cause your service to be shut down until it is located and repaired. It is also a good idea to have this done on a routine basis to avoid potential problems.

24. **Fire Hydrants:** Are they located nearby? A question your insurance company is sure to ask.

25. **Trees:** Many times you will see a park that is full of large beautiful trees and it may look real nice. However, these trees will definitely cost you down the road. You need to keep them trimmed, remove old and dead trees, cleanup the leaves every year, as well as auger sewer lines that become filled with tree roots.

Falling branches are often one of the most likely insurance claims. Also, when you do have these large trees in the park, you want to understand your insurance policy with regards to these. In my experience, when a tree branch or entire tree is blown over the coverage of such event depends on a number of factors. If the tree is healthy and causes damages to an RV or Auto or Mobile Home during a storm, your liability coverage will usually not cover the damage as it will be ruled an "Act of God". However, if the tree is unhealthy or dying, it is more likely that the damage will be covered. However, in that case you may be sued for negligence if you knew about the dying tree and did not take action to have it removed or trimmed. And your insurance company may terminate your future coverage.

26. ***Roads:*** are the roads in good repair, do they need to be re-surfaced, are they wide enough, are there speed bumps, etc? Roads that are not wide enough to maneuver the big RV's in and out of the spaces and those that are not maintained are one of the widespread complaints you will get from your residents and may be a factor that potential RVer's consider when looking for a place to stay.

27. ***Drainage Problems:*** It is advisable to know how an RV Park drains after heavy or sustained rains. Even if the park is not in a flood zone, it can have a horrible problem with standing water and puddles. Getting rid of the excess water can be costly and difficult. Most RVer's will not want to pull into a site that looks more like a lake and not to mention they may be worried about getting stuck.

I made this mistake in a park I purchased in Kentucky. When I conducted my due diligence, it was never raining and I did not notice the problem. About a week after closing I started getting phone calls with people wondering what I was go-ing to do about the water as the previous owner had been promising to fix the problems for years. About a year later I ended up spending over $25,000 on culverts, gravel, and dirt to resolve the worst of the problem.

Here again, if you talk to the permanent residents or some of the prior visitors, they will volunteer much more information than will the seller.

28. **Sewer Plants:** when an RV Park has an actual sewer system, lagoon, or is on septic this is another area in which you should definitely find out as much as possible. You want to know how the system operates, whether it is meeting the EPA guidelines, what it costs to run, what upgrades have been made, whether it is running at full capacity, do you need to have a licensed operator, how many hookups it is licensed for, etc?

This was my $225,000 mistake. I purchased a park in the year 2000 that had its own sewer plant. The park was 61 spaces and had 48 homes in the park. The park had a licensed operator and he claimed that the plant was doing fine. The plant was only a few years old and it was meeting all of the requirements of the state.

I proceeded to fill the park up and with the increased load on the sewer plant, it was no longer meeting the standards set by the state. Not only was I left with the task of trying to fix the problems with the plant, I received a notice that I had to reduce the number of homes in the park back to 48 as this was the maximum number of connections I was allowed. Even after removing the required number of homes, the plant continued to not perform. I spent about $50,000 on ideas suggested by engineers and so called experts to no avail. I was paying about $300 per week just to haul the sewage off and it still didn't work.

Finally, after trying everything we could come up with, I proceeded to replace the current plant with a new one. In the process we were able to increase the number of allowed connections up to 61, but with engineering, permits, and construction, it cost another $175,000 just to have a functioning sewer plant.

29. **Lift Stations:** Are they adequate, do they have warning lights, are there backup pumps?

30. **Investigating the Property:** Walk property during the day and at night. You will uncover many problems such as smells, dog barking, parties, hidden trash & junk, water leaks, sewage puddles, old electrical boxes

31. **Water Wells:** If the park is on wells that are operated by the park, then you will want to find out about the how the system works. Is there more than one well, is there backup pumps in case one of the pumps goes out. In addition, you should find out how deep the wells are and whether this is typical for the area. Also, look at the water pressure, any prior violations or problems, and what it costs to operate. In many cities and states, you will be required to become a certified operator or you will need to employ a certified operator. The function of the certified operator is to take the required water tests and monitor the system to make sure it is operating as it should. If you are planning on becoming the certified operator, then you should check into what educational and other requirements are to become licensed. If you are planning on hiring a certified operator it is a good idea to get multiple quotes and check with the state and make sure they are actually certified. If you are buying a park in an area that has only one or two certified operators, you may want

to have a backup plan in case they start raising their prices or decide to retire or move away. You will also want to find out what the capacity of the well is, as well as how much water you have the rights to use for each well or property. In some areas, you are only allowed to use a certain number of gallons per month or year. Wells and their capacity are designed to handle a certain number of sites and if the well is inadequate to handle the current or future volume, you will want to look at your alternatives (city water, additional wells, etc).

32. **Who is Responsible:** Who pays what? In the typical RV Park, the owner collects a nightly or weekly rate and then provides the utilities. Sometimes, the RV Park will charge additional fees for larger rigs, extra people, pets, cable tv, wireless internet, telephone, etc. You will want to go into detail with the seller and see exactly who is paying what, what amenities are included and which are in addition to the base rates. Also, in RV & MH parks that are renting on a more long term basis, it is not uncommon for the water and electric to be either submetered by the park or else metered directly by the utility companies. One of the biggest keys in looking at the expenses in an RV Park is to dig in deep and find out what all the owners, managers, and maintenance personnel are doing on a day to day basis in the operations of the park. If you are buying from an owner that does all the plumbing, electrical, and other maintenance work and you will not be doing this yourself, you need to make a note of this and adjust your anticipated expenses accordingly. Many times you will find an owner that is very handy and even though he may know more than most electricians and plumbers, he is not licensed to do this type of work and does so under the radar of the

authorities. Another expense that I have seen many times in the past that was way understated is the trash expense. Believe it or not, instead of hiring a company to haul the trash out of the park once or twice a week, the owner loads it up on his pickup and hauls it to the dump (hopefully not to some back country road). I doubt that most people will look forward to doing this project once a week so this expense may need to be adjusted.

33.   ***History of Rate Increases:*** Have the daily, weekly, monthly, and seasonal rates being charged increased consistently over the past years to keep competitive with other competing parks. If you are purchasing a park that has rents that resemble the rates in 1970 and should be raised accordingly and the park is priced based on the lower rates, then you may have a great opportunity to increase the income as well as the value of the park by raising the rates to the market levels.

34.   ***Count the Lots:*** When you are looking at an RV Park to buy and you are told by the owner it has "X" many lots and he shows you on a map that they go up to "X", it is a good idea to actually walk around with the map and list of lots and count them and look at each lot more closely. You will often find that one RV is taking 2 lots, as well as some of the lots are big enough for a small tent or Van but would never be large enough to hold a 32' fifth wheel. You should take the map and a measuring wheel and go around and draw your own map and get the dimensions of each lot so you actually know what you are buying as well what size the spaces are when it comes to renting them to RVers'. In addition, just because the last lot ends in the number "X", does not mean there are that many lots in the park. Many parks have weird

numbering schemes whereby odd numbers are skipped, lots numbers have been consolidated or left out for one reason or another. .

35. *Fees:* Especially in parks whereby lots are rented out for longer terms, you will want to take a look at the bank deposits and compare with the rent roll. When are the rents coming in, are late fees being charged?

36. *Security and Reservation Deposits:* You will want to get a certified list of Security Deposits and Reservation Deposits from the owner. At closing, the buyer is typically credited with this amount. This list will be important in the future when people ask for their security deposits back upon moving out as well as asking you to credit their reservation deposit against the actual camping fees that are charged upon their arrival. If later on, someone claims to have a deposit that is not on that list you have it in writing from the owner.

37. *Check the Leases:* if the park has leases or other rental agreements, then you will want to look for any strange language in these agreements. Are they month to month. Are there long term leases that will make it difficult to raise rents or submeter water?

38. *Hazardous Materials:* don't even consider buying a park without having a Phase 1 environmental study done. If there are any underground storage tanks, above ground storage tanks, chemical drums, buried waste, lagoons, stained soil, gas pumps, auto repair shops, electrical transformers, asbestos in building, etc., you may be liable to the US Government for millions in cleanup costs. For usually $1,500-$2,500 you

can hire a company to conduct this Phase 1 Environmental study and reduce your potential risks tremendously.

39. ***Other Items:*** While this is common sense, it is also easily overlooked or forgotten. When you are looking at a park to buy and something seems odd or just doesn't seem right, then you should investigate. There are hundreds of oddities from park to park and the more you know about them up front the better off you will be whether in your negotiations or dealing with them as the new owner. A couple of brief examples: In one park, I noticed a couple of homes that had extension cords running all over the place. After doing some investigating, many of the electric boxes were not working and people were getting their electric from 2 & 3 spaces over. Definite Hazard. In another case, while walking around the park and looking at the spaces, I noticed that many of the sewer drains were full of rocks and dirt and after pulling up some of the sewer caps, they were also full of debris. By seeing this problem, I was able to have the owner/seller repair this problem before buying the park saving a couple of thousand of dollars. When you have a park with a lot of kids or devious adults, it is a good idea to cap off the sewer lines and even make them child proof if possible. Also, when looking at the park, check into the easements and especially those that may seem strange. People may have given away any number of property rights over the years.

40. ***Recent Survey:*** It is also advisable to obtain a current or recent survey of the park. You want to be sure you are buying what you think you are buying. Are some of RV's or Mobile homes over the property line? Are there fences or sheds over the property lines? With a new owner, the adjoining land

owners may use this time to enforce some of these issues. Check the legal description with the survey and with your contract and warranty deed.

I was brokering a Park deal in Greeley, Colorado about a month after I received my real estate license. Needless to say, the park was 3 separate parcels and at closing, the buyer received a deed for only one of the parcels. Neither I, the buyer, the seller, nor Title Company caught the mistake and a few months later the issue came up when the buyer was refinancing the property. The buyer owned about a third of the park. If it had not been for the fact that the Sellers were honest people and signed the paperwork to transfer the other 2 parcels of land to the buyer at no charge, I would have been in trouble for not doing my job in a diligent manner.

41. *Current Zoning:* Seller says the property can be expanded. Make sure the current zoning will allow the proposed expansion. Also make sure that it is feasible: Where can you tap into the water, sewer, and other utilities? Do the current water wells and sewer plant have the capability to service additional hookups? What are the impact fees? What are the likely costs to expand?

42. *Lot Sizes:* one of the biggest issues with older RV and Mobile Home Parks is that they were built for smaller RV's and Mobile Homes of the 1960's & 1970's. Just as the slogan goes "Everything is bigger in Texas", so it goes with today's RV's & Mobile Homes. They have constantly become bigger and bigger. As they have continued to get bigger, these smaller lots will not handle them. In many cases, the parks have to either use 2 spaces to service one hookup or else reconfigure the entire park. I have seen many parks that fill up their pull

through and larger back in spaces on a consistent basis night after night. However, they have 20 or so other spaces that are smaller and will not handle these larger RV.s. So while they still have vacancies, they have to turn away potential customers because many of the sites are obsolete for todays RV's. On the mobile home side of it, you will often run into the same problem in that your spaces were built for the 12' x 60' homes and the new homes are 16' x 80' and bigger. To complicate it even more, many cities/counties are requiring mobile homes that are being moved into their city/county to be of a certain age (10 or 20 years old maximum) and it can be difficult finding homes that fit this criteria as well as people that want to live in these smaller homes. Thus, moving an older 12' x 50' home into your park may not be an option.

43. ***Other Site Issues:*** so you have taken your map around and measured all the lots and are comfortable with the number of sites and sizes of those sites. However, now you should also check out each of those sites and see what services are going to each of them. Do they have water, sewer, electric, gas, phone, cable, etc? Are these services actually working at these sites? Are the water and sewer lines marked? Is there gas and electric? Does the electric need to be upgraded before accepting a modern RV. What are the setback requirements? Are the lots in such an arrangement where an RV can actually be placed into each lot without moving other RV's or homes around?

44. ***Combination Parks:*** When you are dealing with a combination Mobile Home and RV Park or else a seasonal RV park with permanent units (RV's or Park Models), you will want

to make sure these permanent units are tied down according to the Standards set by the State or County regulations. Many older parks have units that are in there and were never installed properly including being tied down according to code if even at all. I have experienced this twice in the past. One time a tornado hit one of my parks (actually 2 parks next to each other). All in all we lost over 40 homes out of 100 and the homes that were actually tied down and installed correctly were much less damaged than the ones that were not. Another time we had some high winds in one of my parks and 2 of the homes just blew over as they were not tied down.

45. **Street Lights:** drive through the park at night and see how well the park is lighted. Are there problem areas? You will also want to find out who is responsible for the street light maintenance as well as keeping working bulbs in them. Many cases, you will pay a monthly fee to the electric company and they will maintain the lights completely. Other times, you will be blessed with the responsibility of maintaining the lights and changing the bulbs. It is not fun changing light bulbs 20+ feet in the air and can be costly to hire it done (probably worth the price though unless you have a bucket truck)..

46. **Plat Maps:** If at all possible get a plat map. If one is not available ask the owner to draw one to the best of his knowledge and locate any cleanouts, shutoffs, etc. This is important to have in case of line breaks and other emergencies in the future. The seller or property manager that has been there for a several years knows every in and out of the park and tapping into that knowledge as much as possible during your due

diligence period will make your life much easier if you understand most of what is going on and where everything is.

47. **Park Equipment:** Does the park have adequate equipment to operate? If the current owner has a pickup, tractor, mower, make sure to negotiate for this as it will come in handy in the future and you don't want to have to start buying all of this the month you take over. It is a good idea to get a list of all the supplies and equipment currently being used to operate the park and have it included in the purchase.

48. **Market Survey:** Find out what other parks are charging and make sure to find out what they are charging for. One park may pay all the utilities while another park may have a base rate and then add on charges for everything whether through submetering or charging by the person, etc. You want to compare apples to apples. One thing that I would suggest is to not talk to other park owners in the area until you have the property under contract. Many times, they are looking to expand and as soon as you hang up with them they will be on their way to see the owner of the park you are trying to buy. However, these other park owners can provide insight into the area, market, and information on the park you are buying such as reputation, how it has been managed, etc. If they say something bad about the park, you should investigate further because once again, they might be wanting to buy it from under you or else they are so proud of their own park that everything else is less than mediocre..

In addition to comparing other parks in your market, you may find that some of these parks cater to families, some to those people that are 55 and over and some may be catering to construction workers and the list goes on. You might find that the park that you are looking at may cater to one of these classes of people (as long as it is legal and doing so in a non-discriminatory manner). In addition, it is becoming more common for parks to cater to certain classes and price ranges of motorhomes. The idea is to make sure that the park is operating as it should and whether it services the general public or a specific group.

49. ***Building and Zoning:*** Visit the planning department to see if there are any new parks that are going to be built as well as the location of any vacant land zoned for RV Park development. If a brand new park is in the works nearby you will want to investigate the positive/negative effects of such a new development.

50. ***Long-term Resident Issues:*** For parks with long term residents you will want to find out the eviction laws for that state/county/city. Some states tend to be pro landlord and some pro resident. You should educate yourself on the whole eviction process and whether you will be able to go through the process yourself or if you will need to hire an attorney to do it for you. In some cases, you might be able to find an attorney that will help you through the first one or two and then you can take it from there. A great source of information would be other park owners/managers and apartment owners/managers in the area. Chances are they will have been through the process and can give you valuable information from their experiences.

51. ***Zoning:*** You should check with the local zoning department in order to find out what the current zoning is on the property you are buying. In some cases, the zoning will have changed and the park is grandfathered in. The important

aspect of this process is to make sure that the current uses are legal and within the zoning law.

52. **City Utilities:** if your park is currently using wells and/or septics then it would be good to know when and if city/public utilities are likely to be made available to the property. Also, if a city has extended or is going to extend utilities to your location are you required to hook on and if so at what cost?

53. **The Junk Collector:** Removing Old Junk Piles, RV's, and Mobile Homes – In reviewing the property, you will often find sellers that have accumulated their own junk as well as others. Most buyers go in with the mindset that they want to clean up the park and improve its appearance. I usually try to insert a stipulation in the contract or as part of my due diligence to have the the Seller remove major junk piles, old RV's, abandoned mobile homes, junk cars, etc. These items can often be costly to move and your money is better spent on other improvements.

54. **Rental Units:** If the park you are buying has rental units (RV's, Mobiles, Cabins) or rent-to-own units, make every effort to check these out. You will not only see how the units are being taken care of by the residents, you will also get an indication of the way the current owner runs his business. If you find holes or soft spots in the floor or walls, bad carpeting jobs and such, this may be an indication that the owner is not only doing quick fixes on the homes but also in the park maintenance as well.

I have seen this many times in the past. I buy a park that has some rental units and the renters start calling to say they were promised all kinds of repairs by the previous owner. I have been in homes where there is mold on the walls, 2 foot diameter holes in the floor, buckets collecting water from leaks in the ceiling and so on. It is better to know up front what you are dealing with.

The more thorough you are in the due diligence phase, the better you will understand the property as well as the potential problems that may occur specific to the property. In addition, you will be much more comfortable when taking over the property and most likely have plumbers, electricians, and other contractors on board to aid you in the future.

When doing your due diligence, there are some things that you just cannot change and the risk will just be too high to proceed. Other things may just be too costly. Other areas of the due diligence may discover smaller problems that you should be able to change with proper management and operations and can lead to quick equity and profit increases.

If this is your first park or you would rather have an experienced professional help you in the process, contact us and we can provide a recommendation. While it may seem expensive to pay a couple of thousand dollars to have an expert evaluate your proposed purchase, they can usually find things that you can go back to the seller and renegotiate and save several times more than the fee you paid.

RV Park Financing

If you have average to excellent credit it is not difficult to locate financing for cars, boats, homes, duplexes, apartments, and unsecured credit lines. However, when you enter into the world of seeking financing for RV Parks you will most likely endure some frustrations. Many banks have those types of loans that they will not make and RV Parks will often fall into that category.

It has been my experience that the smaller the loan amount the less options you will have. In addition, loans for RV parks that are run down, underperforming, or do not have a good financial history are even more difficult to obtain.

You may have banked with the same bank for many years and built a great relationship with them. However, when you tell them you are quitting your job and buying an RV park they all of a sudden lose their comfort level. You will have to educate them and show them that you understand how to operate an RV park.

In most cases with RV Parks you will usually need to obtain financing from the seller, a local bank with whom you have a relationship with or a local bank in the same market as the property, or private and hard money lenders. The key is to not give up in your search. When seeking out lenders to finance the park, try to find banks and lenders that have successfully loaned on parks in the past. If they have had a good experience with other similar loans, it will be much easier to get the loan approved and funded.

Credible lenders do not make money unless they are able to get the deal done and so it is to their benefit as well as yours to get the loan closed and funded. You might have to help push the deal through and one of the best ways to do so is to have a well prepared and realistic business plan that you submit to the lender with the application. I am attaching a sample business plan at the end of this book.

I have never been turned down for a loan when I have presented this business plan to a qualified potential lender.

When lenders are evaluating your loan request they complete a due diligence of sorts themselves. Some of the important points they are looking to satisfy in this process are:

- Researching you as the borrower… your credit report and rating, your financial statements, your overall business experience and your experience with Real Estate and RV Parks, if any.

- Does the loan request meet the bank's lending guidelines? Is the loan to value, debt coverage ratios and loan amount all within their guidelines?

- Is the loan officer and underwriter experienced enough in real estate and particularly with RV Parks and Campgrounds to recognize any of the hidden risks that may occur?

- If the property does go through foreclosure, what is going to be the banks exit policy? How long will it take to market it, what can the buyer do to harm the value, and what is the likely price the property can be sold for to satisfy the remaining mortgage?

- If the bank does not want to hold it in their portfolio, who will the bank sell it to and is it within the guidelines of who they will sell it to?

If you can concentrate on finding out what these guidelines are for the bank and then customizing your loan request to fit within these guidelines, you will have a much better chance of successfully getting the loan closed. In addition, addressing any of these other issues that the bank is going to struggle with before they come up will also increase your chances. If you qualify the bank you are applying with before going through the process, you will save a lot of time if you know the bank does lend on RV Parks and does have a loan program that will fit your needs as the purchaser.

Another option to finance RV Park is to look for SBA (Small Business Administration) loans. These loans are made by many local banks but are different in that they are backed by the U.S. Government. Applying for and obtaining an SBA loan is a lengthy and detailed process but it can be worth the time if the other options are not panning out.

No matter what type of financing you obtain, you will generally be making a down payment in the 20-30 percent range with the loan amortized over 20 to 30 years.

There are several lenders on RVParkStore.com that specialize in the industry and will guide you through the process. Here are a few potential lenders:

Company	Contact	Phone
CampgroundFinancing.com	Jerry Persons	877-569-5691 x 301
NicheLend	Frank Twohig	800-590-9840
Liberty Funding	Anita Huedepohl	800-975-2691
Nationwide Commercial Funding	Robert Lucci	941-921-0000
PMC Commercial Trust	Mary Brownmiller	972-349-3209
Creative Commercial Lending	Russ Thompson	781-837-1165
Wells Fargo Commercial Mortgage	Eric Khoa	760-438-2153
GLM Commercial	Gary La Mantia	800-303-6473
Bond Street Capital Commercial Mortgage	Jeff Moss	818-865-4100

Here is a sample program that is being offered through a company called Nichelend:

Maximum Loan to Value of 75 Percent
ARM's: 6 month, 2/28, 3/27 and 7/23
Amortizations: 15, 20, or 30 year
Balloons: None
Income underwriting method: DTI (debt to income – based on borrower not property)
Minimum Loan Amount: $100,000
Maximum Loan Amount: $1,500,000

There are several types of lenders out there as well as several different types of loans. The common types of Lenders are:

- **Banks** – loans are typically are based on your relationship with them and require you to personally guarantee the loan.

- **Credit Companies** – they are typically portfolio or conduit lenders and depending on the property type and borrower's credentials the loan may be recourse or non-recourse

- **Hard Money Lenders** – this is an expensive source of capital and is usually only used for short time frames – the rates are higher and the loan to values are lower, but an otherwise impossible deal is often made possible through these types of lenders.

- **Investment Banks** – these types of banks do large transactions – 2 million and up – they have strict underwriting requirements and are typically non-recourse loans

- **Life Companies** – this type of lender is looking for the large loans on the premium properties – the interest rates are usually the best out there and they have strict lending requirements but well worth it if you are looking to hold long term and you fit into their program.

- **Mortgage Brokers** – they are not lenders but if they are experienced with RV Parks, they often have great sources to find you the best program to fit your needs. You pay them usually one or two points to be on your side and get your deal done.

- **Private Money Lenders** – the last resort and you definitely want to have an attorney review any documentation you sign. The rates are usually very high and each lender has its own way of doing things. However, they can help you in very hard to finance properties.

Here are the basic types of loans:

- **Conduit Loans** – these loans are based on the property more than the borrower. They are non-recourse and usually have prepayment penalties and more documentation and loan costs. However the interest rates and other terms are usually better.

- **Portfolio Loans** – these loans are based on the borrower as well as the property. They are recourse but usually more flexible. The documentation is simpler and the loan closing costs are usually less. However the terms and interest rates are not as favorable as conduit loans.

Why would a seller finance the park rather than taking all cash? There are several reasons but the most common are:

- They can often get 10% or more from the sale in selling price.

- Quicker Closings.

- Bank and outside financing is much harder to obtain and they could lose many otherwise qualified buyers. They want to sell!

- Deferring of a portion of capital gains.

- Higher interest rate in terms of holding a note as compared to putting it in the bank or a CD. They may be able to borrow against the note.

- Comfort level with the value of the park – they feel the park is worth more than what they are financing and if the buyer defaults they can always take it back and resell it again. This also gives the buyer an added comfort level in that they will feel like the seller believes in the park.

RV Park Insurance and Risk Management:

First of all, I want to thank my good friend and insurance professional, Kurt Kelley, for his assistance in writing this section. Kurt has been writing insurance for us for several years. Kurt and his associates understand the business and can provide you with valuable assistance in selecting the right insurance policy for your property. Here is Kurt's contact information:

Mobile Insurance Agency	Kurt Kelley	281-367-9266 x17

The Number 1 thing with insurance and risk management is to make sure you limit your susceptibility to losses. Always work with an insurance agent that understands RV Parks and Campgrounds and can help you reduce these risks.

When you are evaluating an RV Park or Campground to purchase you should receive a Profit and Loss Statement from the owner and on that should be a line item for insurance. Many times when you dig deeper into the numbers, you will find that the insurance figure not only includes the insurance for the park and contents, but also on the owner's personal autos and even health insurance. You want to separate these "extra" coverages when you are evaluating the property.

Also, when evaluating the park you should get a quote from a proven company that understands RV Parks and the risks involved. When buying liability and property coverage's it is not a good idea to base this decision on price alone. You want to read the fine print.

I was involved in a park several years ago that was hit by a tornado and one of the thoughts I had was I hope that my insurance would kick in and cover the damage. I had a similar experience when a park I had just sold was affected in 2006 by Hurricane Rita. Here are some of the things I learned the hard way after turning in the claims hoping to get coverage:

Loss of Income Coverage: This is one of those standard or extra coverage's you find offered from insurance companies. The idea is that if your property is damaged by a fire, flood, tornado or other disaster, then you will receive money from the insurance company to offset some of the loss of business. There are many types of Loss of Income/Rents coverage's out there and when I had the tornado hit my park I found out quickly some of the problems with my Loss of Income policy. Basically, the insurance company said that I was to be compensated on each lot that had been rented out and that was damaged and not rentable for up to a year. Here is the kicker… once we cleaned up the lots and they were once again rentable plus 30 days (time put into operation plus 30 days) the coverage would stop! Even though I had a renter on that lot before the tornado and their home was destroyed, I would not receive my 12 months of loss of rents unless I left the lot in a not rentable condition.

"Extended Indemnity" – this type of coverage will cost extra, but it will cover the lease-up period while you try to renew a leaseable lot.

"Extra Expense" – this type of coverage will also cost extra, but it can pay to remove debris from a lot so that it becomes leaseable.

Property Coverage's: Typically when you are buying a park that has Recreational Halls, Owners Quarters, and other buildings you will typically list each one of these and insure it. However, there are many other infrastructure items that you may not even think about. When the parks were damaged from the tornado and hurricane, there was damage to other areas of the infrastructure that was not covered. Many of the electric and water lines were destroyed and there was a nice 8 foot cedar fence running around 3 sides of one of the parks. When the park was hit by the tornado there was no coverage for the utility lines that were damaged. This cost about $45,000 to fix. Then a few years and many policies later, I was usually getting coverage to cover the utilities in case of a national disaster. However, when the hurricane hit the park near Beaumont, and did some damage to one of the buildings that was insured it was covered by the policy. However there was this 8 foot cedar fence that was completely destroyed and I had never even thought about insuring that. Come to find out the insurance would have cost only a couple of hundred dollars more per year and it would have covered that $20K loss. Even though most fence and utility pole losses are small, if you are located in hazardous wind areas, you should insure them because of the total damage such wind storms can cause.

When you are buying a park the key is to look around at the entire park and ask yourself what could happen in the case of a natural disaster and then get quotes on each specific aspect and then decide on the risks you are willing to take. If you want to save on premiums you should consider higher deductibles as opposed to not insuring fences, utility poles, signs, etc.

When searching for insurance for your RV Park, you will want to make sure the company you are considering understands the business as well as the potential liabilities and risks involved. You should ask them as many questions as you can and see how they respond. Then check the fine print and make sure their answers are not contradictory to the fine print. Once again, the insurance companies on our website have knowledge of the industry and will be able to provide you with a good policy that will cover you for the standard losses as well as for additional exposures specific to RV Parks.

Some of the factors that affect your insurance rates include:

- Your experience in the industry and history of claims/losses

- The property size and condition

- Adequacy of lighting

- Additional exposures such as swimming pools, playgrounds, and other property specific exposures – including park owned homes

- Property location and susceptibility to crime, hurricanes, tornados, etc.

- Types of utilities provided and whether public or private, above or below ground, etc.

In addition, if you have RV's, Cabins, Motel Rooms, or Mobile Homes that you rent out, the general park liability policy will not cover these so you need to get a separate or additional policy for liability as well as physical coverage. Make sure your residents have insurance on their homes – especially in flood, hurricane, and tornado areas. If possible, have them name you as an "additional insured" on their debris removal coverage so that you aren't stuck with that expense if their home is damaged and remains in the park.

Back to my experience with the tornado: In October of 2001, my family and I were taking a vacation in Florida and about half way through that vacation, I received a call that 2 of my parks located adjacent to each other in Texas were just hit by a tornado. Needless to say of the 100 or so homes in the park, about 40 were damaged beyond repair. It was truly an experience I will never forget. Besides the fact that we just lost almost 50% of our income, we had 40 homes to remove. Of these 40 homes, about 10 of the residents had insurance that covered the removal of the homes and 3 residents paid out of their pocket to remove their homes. The rest of the people just walked away and left us with the cost and responsibility to clean up the lots. Needless to say, we now try to require all homeowners to carry insurance on their homes. Some insurance companies also offer non-owned home debris removal which is a great coverage for park owners.

Closing Checklist

- Get Insurance (property and liability).

- For long term residents: Obtain Estoppel Certificates which show lease commencement and expiration dates, rent payment status (current or past due), security deposit, defaults by landlord, modifications or amendments to the lease.

- Transfer Utilities – get all phone numbers and account numbers from seller. Find out what deposits are required, etc.

- Transfer Advertising – contact travel directories (Woodall's, Trailer Life, etc) to get listed or else transfer listing to new ownership. In addition, contact telephone companies to transfer yellow page ads as well as any state highway signs and billboards.

- Transfer or apply for any other licenses you will need to continue the park operations (restaurant, liquor, marina, boat, guide service).

- Apply for a Sales Tax Permit.

- Get as much information available from prior owner on past guests. You can use this list as well as build your own to write letters, emails, and other contact opportunities to let them know of the new ownership as well as special promotions and events.

- Get contractors lined up and negotiate fees in advance – get certicates of liability insurance. Whether you are lining up contractors for improvement work or routine plumbing and electrical maintenance it is best to have them lined up and familiar with you when you are ready for them and especially in an emergency.

- Get bank account setup, order checks, and deposit slips. In addition, you will want to open up a merchant account that will allow you to take payments by credit cards.

- Get all records for management & maintenance personnel and get signed employment or independent contractor letters from each of them.

- Arrange Workers compensation insurance.

- Get current rent roll showing any delinquent rents.

- Obtain forms – check in sheets, leases, rules, and all other forms that are needed to run the business.

Other RV Park Considerations

Low Occupancy/High Vacancy:

Potential reasons for this include: new parks, poorly managed parks, parks with rents too high, bad infrastructure, poor reputation, and usually a bad local economy - decide which of these factors are the cause and decide which ones you can change. You can't change everything overnight and some things no matter what you do, you will not be able to change.

Private vs Public Utilities:

The best scenario is a park on city services with the lines owned and maintained by the city.

Next would be a park on city services in which the city owns the lines up to the park connection.

Then a park on private utilities that is operating smoothly and at a reasonable cost AND that has the ability to connect to city services in the case of a problem at a reasonable rate.

Next would be a park with private utilities that are operating within limits and capacity.

Lastly would be a park on private utilities that is experiencing problems. Parks with bad water wells or sewer systems can be a nightmare as the costs and time to repair or replace are usually high and can go on for months.

Also, if a city has extended or is going to extend utilities to your location are you required to hook on and if so at what cost?

In the past several years, many laws and regulations both Federal and State are making it much more difficult to operate your own utilities in an efficient and cost effective manner.

Amenities: When evaluating an RV park you will want to look at the current amenities as well as the cost and benefits of these amenities. If you are operating a park that caters to overnight campers, then you can usually get by with fewer amenities than if you are operating a park that is catering to those who stay for a week or month at a time. Ultimately I would rather have a park that rents the land and is not filled with amenities (clubhouses, swimming pools, etc). The reason for this is that these amenities cost you money to operate and maintain and there is usually only a small percentage of your guests that will use them anyways. In some cases you may lose business because you don't have a swimming pool, exercise room, shuffleboard, or whatever. However, this is usually not the case. If you are operating a park that caters to longer term residents, to keep them there and coming back, you may have to have additional amenities to be successful.

One note on Membership type RV parks and campgrounds: I have seen many of these types of parks that start out great with nice amenities and service. They start selling memberships to everyone they can get into the park and then as these membership sales start to slow down, so does the maintenance of the park and the service to existing members. I have talked with hundreds of people that have purchased memberships in these types or parks and have seen them gradually become run down year after year.

Park Owned RVs, Mobiles, or Cabins: When considering operating a park and having park owned rental homes, if you are not operating the park yourself then you will most likely need enough homes to keep a part or full time maintenance person busy. If you do not have staff on site it will usually be cost prohibitive to hire plumbers, carpenters, and other contractors to do all the repairs on the homes. In order to justify having rentals I would estimate you should have at least 20 if not more in order to make to keep a maintenance staff.

Managing an RV Park:

Once you purchase the park you will have ideas and strategies to implement and the only way to find out if they work is to try them and then try variations of them to make it better, and keep testing and modifying as you go. What may work today may not work next month. Be flexible but diligent.

Your goal in managing your RV Park is to rent out every space you can when you are open, rent your spaces at the rate you feel is fair and acceptable, keep the property maintained and running smoothly, reduce your expenses as much as possible, keep the guests happy so they keep coming back, make your guests feel like they are getting an adequate service for what they are paying, and reduce your liability exposure.

When taking over an RV Park, it is important to take the previous system that was in place and adjust it to make it work for you. In one of the RV Parks I owned, the prior ownership kept business hours from 9:00 am to 5:00 pm and was available during those times to check in new guests, sell items in the store, etc. However, they had no system to check people in after 5:00 pm so they were losing many late arriving guests. We immediately installed check in slips with instructions on where to park, etc and this helped cater to those guests that arrived late.

Here are a few other thoughts on management.

- When you are looking to purchase an RV Park or Campground to run yourself or as a family business you will have to decide on whether you will hire full or part-time employees and workcampers. If you are going to run the entire operation without any other help, you may want to consider at least having someone familiar enough with park that can handle it for you while you are on vacation or have an emergency. RV Parks usually require someone onsite to operate it and handle emergencies. If you try to do too much without any time off, you are likely to become burnt out.

- If you decide to hire full or part-time employees you will have many of the same problems as do other hospitality and cash businesses. You want to come up with a way to track the cash and other money coming in and out to discourage as well as detect theft. Remember to check with the laws of the state or locality to abide with minimum wages, payroll taxes, workers compensation and other nuances with running a business with employees.

- A popular option in obtaining help with office and/or maintenance work is to use the services of workcampers or camp hosts. These are usually full time or seasonal RVer's that will work in exchange for the rent and utilities. In some cases, they will also be paid on an hourly or salary basis in addition to the rent and utilities. This often helps to supplement their income as well as keeping them busy and feeling useful. In many cases, they will have a many technical skills such as plumbing, electrical, carpentry, cement, and when you need this type of work done, they can do it better than many local contractors and at reduced prices. There are many opportunities in the use of workcampers.

- Raising rates – you want to evaluate your daily, weekly, monthly rates on a regular basis and you want to make sure that your rates go up faster than your expenses are increasing. After all, most people are in the business to make a profit and if you wait too long to raise your rates you will be missing out. For monthly or seasonal rates, it is a good idea to raise the rents every year in order to get it into the minds of the residents. There is much less resistance when they expect it even if it is just a couple of dollars.

- If the park you are buying is mainly seasonal or monthly and is nearly full, then in most cases, you should immediately raise rents – the residents will expect it. The opposite is true. If the park is a turnaround park with high vacancy then instead of raising rents you might consider offering big incentives to current and potential residents in order to get the park filled.

- If you are going to manage the park, it will be good to keep some distance in order to not get personally involved with the residents. This usually leads to problems and favors. It is hard to say no if you become to close.

- When we were running our first park in Limon we had our kids at the park many times and they naturally played with some of the kids in the park. Then they started wanting to have sleepovers, etc and it became increasingly difficult to be strict on the parents when their kids were friends with ours..

- What do you pay a manager? I get asked this question a lot and usually respond with: What your feel is reasonable. A full time manager or fee based management company will usually get in the range of 5-10% of the gross income plus free lot rent. I think a lot of it has to do with what the manager is doing to earn his money. You can often times check with other area RV parks, Hotels and Motels, and other similar businesses and get an idea of what they are paying and try to stay in that range..

- If the park is stable and operating smoothly and the manager is just checking in guests and doing minor maintenance the amount may be as low as 5-6%. If the manager is working 40 hours a week, plus being on call for emergencies, it may be that it is closer to 10-12%.

- When you have a good manager that is doing a great job, it will pay to keep them happy and not looking for another job.

- A good manager and your oversight of that manager is probably the most important aspect of running a park to the best of its potential.

Increasing the Value and Profitability of Your RV Park:

1. *Raise Rates:* Whether daily, weekly, monthly or seasonal, an increase in rates without a drop in occupancy will increase the value of a park. Collecting $1 more per space for an average of 10 days a month using a valuation based on a 10% capitalization rate, can increase the per lot value by $1,200. Other increases such as charging more for pets, additional people, telephone, cable, wi-fi are also possible. I have seen many parks in which the rates have been the same for many years. The owners may own the park free and clear and rather than upset the returning guests and permanent residents they opt to keep the rates the same. They may be making

enough money to live as they desire and that is completely understandable. The problem you usually run into is that these same owners want to base the value and sales price of the park on the market rates rather than the rates they are charging. Most of the time when you buy a park, the residents expect a raise, so don't let them down!

2.   ***Submeter Water and Sewer and Trash:*** For RV Parks with monthly or seasonal spaces, you can install water meters and start billing the residents back for water and sewer and trash which will in effect increase your bottom line. I often think this is one of the most equitable ways to pass on expenses to the residents as they only pay for what they use. In my experience when meters have been installed the master water and sewer bill is reduced by 30-40% as your residents become conscious about the amount of water going through the faucets. Leaky faucets are fixed, toilets no longer run continually; cars are not washed every day, etc.

3.   ***Enforce Rules and Leases:*** By enforcing reasonable rules and regulations your RV Park will be regarded as a safe and comfortable environment. When people pull up to stay for the night, and they see trash or hear loud and obnoxious music, they may very well move on down the road to the next park. Get rid of problem tenants. If you are worried about losing the rent from one or two problem residents, consider that you may lose even more good residents and potential residents by keeping those that are causing problems and not obeying the rules.

4.   ***Reduce your Property Tax Expense:*** Contact a company that specializes in going to bat for you with your county tax assessor to get your valuation and taxes reduced. Many states

and counties base the assessed value on the purchase price. However, RV Parks have a large business value component that should not be taxed as real property tax. These companies often work for a percent of the reduced taxes thus no money out of pocket expenses if they are unsuccessful. Here is a link to a website in which you can find companies that specialize in this field.

http://aptcnet.com/members.html

5. ***Reduce other ongoing expenses:*** Get multiple insurance quotes, evaluate telephone costs and extras, negotiate with plumbers and electricians to get a lower hourly rate, etc.

6. ***Rent More Overnight Spaces and fill vacant monthly lots:*** Obviously the more paying guests you have the more your income will be and in turn your net profits should be higher as well. There are many ways to bring in additional guests to your park including camp directory advertising, magazine advertising, direct mail, billboard advertising, and internet advertising. Advertising in RV Directories is a must to get those people that plan ahead to schedule a stop at your park. If you are looking for additional guests then you should try these other methods of advertising and make sure you track the different types of campaigns you are conducting to see which ones work, which ones need tweaked, and which ones are not worth the money. If you just start throwing ads around without a system to track them, you will most likely be throwing money away on campaigns that don't work and not spending enough money on the campaigns that work. If you have a combination RV/MH park or seasonal spaces with mobiles or park models and you have vacant lots that could be filled, then you should think about how much those

vacant lots are worth? In many cases, a vacant lot is actually costing you money to keep the grass mowed, the lot clean, and so on. If your lot rent is $200 per month and based on a simple formula that a lot is worth 60 times the monthly rent, then an occupied lot is worth $12,000. Would it make financial sense to spend $2,000 to cover the home moving costs of a potential resident? I believe it does. Other incentives I have used include, free or reduced rent for the first year or two; free installation of new skirting, free steps and decks, and the list goes on. Be creative and stay ahead of your competitors. It is much more effective to come up with 50 ways to market to one customer rather than 1 way to market to 50 customers.

7. ***Buy homes for Resale or Rental.*** Buying used RV's, Park Models, Mobiles, Cabins and placing them in your community for resale or rental is another way to drastically increase the value of your community. As mentioned before, each time you fill a vacant space, the value of your park increases. As a community owner you have an advantage over most mobile home retailers in that you do not need to make a profit on the sale of new and used homes. If you profit by $12,000 per space in equity each time you add a new home, you can sell the homes at breakeven and still be way ahead.

8. ***Section off a portion of your park for Park Models.*** There is a growing trend for people to enjoy an endless summer. They live in warmer southern regions in the south during the winter and up north during the summer. If you section a portion of your park off to cater to these individuals you can realize a year round stabilized income while they are only using your utilities about half the year. There are about 4,000

RV Parks in the country that can handle park models and in most cases, park models are classified as RV's rather than mobile homes that are allowed to be used as part time living quarters. Just be sure to check your local regulations.

9. ***Increase the Curb Appeal:*** With an RV Park, first impressions can make a big difference. When you first pull up to the park, there should be a nice sign and entrance. Planting flowers, bushes and trees to make the entrance look good is important. You do not want the guests to turn around before they enter the park. Nice wide roads that are not full of potholes are important to many people. Most RV's are not 4x4's and I have seen many parks that for a thousand dollars or less could greatly improve the entrance and first impression of the park. In addition to the entrance, you should concentrate on keeping your park clean. On a daily basis you or one of your staff should walk the park and clean up any trash and check out the spaces that were just vacated to make sure everything is clean. Sewer caps should be on or closed, water should be turned off, and so on. You don't want the next person to occupy the lot to have to pick up trash and clean up after the previous guest. A bad impression is a lasting impression! In addition to the cleanliness of the park, it is very important to keep the bathrooms, shower rooms, laundry rooms and any other facilities clean and sanitary. If you have a portion of the park with permanent or extended stay residents, you should encourage them to follow the rules and take pride in there homes and sites. Another important factor is to make sure the property has adequate lighting as well as routinely making sure the bulbs are not burned out. This is not only important for safety and comfort of the guests but can also

reduce your liability. Have new and attractive signs installed at the entrances. Repair roads and maintain adequate street lighting. For longer term residents, have monthly rent discount incentives to the residents for things such as: Property of the month, most improved property, etc. If you can push programs such as these you are basically having your residents improve the property for you! Additionally, financing for your residents such things as new skirting, paint, wood siding, and other outside improvements can get the homes looking better as well.

10. ***Add additional income sources:*** If you have some vacant land, consider adding some mini storage units, or fence it off and offer storage for RV's, Boats, and extra automobiles. Depending on the park, many of the guests may return frequently and having the opportunity to store their RV's, Boats, ATV's, and Cars could be a nice extra profit for you as well as a convenience for them. If you have highway frontage, look into placing billboards or selling easements to billboard companies. Look into getting Cable TV or Wi-Fi for the entire park and in doing so, your residents will get a break on these costs and you should be able to profit as well. Rent out the clubhouse for special events and sell passes to your pool to non residents. Another possibility would be to add a Recreational Vehicle Wash (large car wash). Charging a few extra dollars at check in for a wash could be highly profitable. Other possibilities could include offering fee based dump stations, vehicle repairs, moving of RV's from storage to sites and vice versa.

11. ***Sell New and Used RV's, Park Models, and Mobile Homes.*** As the park owner you will be getting calls from your advertis-

ing already and are in prime position to act as a seller, broker or facilitator to sell RV's, Park Models, and Mobile Homes in your park whether as part of your inventory or those belonging to your current residents. (Make sure to check on state licensing laws)

12. ***Provide leads to residents for insurance, inspections, warranties, and financing.*** You might also take it to the next step and actually offer these services as an authorized representative. Some of the things that I have seen in the past include giving away gift baskets or bags to you guests when they pull up. You might be able to sell advertising on these promotional gifts or some companies that target RVer's may send them to you and have you pass them out for them. If they are actually useful items, then it should be a success. People love to receive gifts and they will remember these little things and pass the word around to their friends and acquaintances. Word of mouth advertising is usually the best type of advertising you can get.

13. ***Set your park apart from the rest.*** Do not just copy everything that everyone else is doing but set your park up as unique in the eyes of the visitor. Of course you want to make sure this uniqueness appeals to your target market and doesn't scare them off.

14. ***Membership Affilitations:*** Another possible way to increase your income is through affiliations with the different RV and Camping Clubs and Membership programs out there. Some of these clubs include Good Sam, Coast-to-Coast, RPI and others. The program basically works like this: you become one of their affilitates and then you are listed in their directories and websites. Then when a member of one of these clubs

visits your park, they often receive a discounted rate. If you are looking for additional guests, this can be a great way to increase your overnight and other traffic.

In addition to becoming affiliated with these clubs, it has become more and more popular in the past whereby RV Parks and Campgrounds have been selling memberships for their park exclusively or amongst several parks. This typically works for the parks that are in destination areas or are the destination themselves. This program typically works like this… You sell a membership to your otherwise overnight guests and then this membership will allow them to stay at your park (or several affiliated parks) for free or discounted rates plus you can charge a yearly maintenance fee. They are typically limited to a specific number of nights per year, as well as limits on the amount of time they can stay in a row (typically 14 days). This type of program can increase your income substantially until you are sold out. The cost of these memberships may be as low as $400 and can go up to $20,000 plus for premier locations. Selling 500 memberships at $2,000 each is a million dollars. Of course you must make sure that you are able to service these memberships and fulfill your contracts with these buyers or you can be in for major problems down the road.

15. ***Internet Marketing.*** Everyone knows that the power of the Internet continues to increase and even though you may not believe it will help your business, there are some things you can and should do to drive new visitors to your park as well as stay in contact with prior visitors. There are all kinds of books and strategies out there to show you how to market on the internet and you will learn a lot from some of these.

If you are looking for suggestions send us and email and we can provide a link to the ones we have read and would recommend.

However, without the full course on Internet Marketing, I believe there are 3 things that are very simple, cheap, and will allow you to grow your business without much effort at all.

- *Website:* you need a website even if it is just a simple one page site with your RV Parks name, address, phone number, and a few photos and directions to your facility. When someone calls you they will often ask if you have a website and whether you have photos, etc. Many of your competitors will have a site and if you do not it can look as if you are behind times. If you do not have any idea of how to create a website or webpage and you do not want to learn, we are able to help you with simple sites or pages for as little as $50.00 per year.

- *Online Reservations:* this is becoming more and more prevalent and if it is feasible for you to start taking online reservations through your website or with web services this can help increase the number of guests that pull in.

- *Links to Your Website:* so you have a website and you need to direct traffic to that site. Here are some very simple strategies to get people to your site: List you park and website on the RVParkStore.com directory for FREE. In addition, go to all the other national websites as well as those in your local area and get your RV Park listed in their directories with a link to your website. Note: when you do get listed on these directories, you will have a much higher response to your listing since you have a website that people can click on and find out more about your park. (It does not have to be a $10,000 site). A simple, clean site with basic information is all that you need to get people to call you.

- *Email Addresses.* Do you like things that are FREE and that are proven to make you MORE MONEY? Well, if you do then should follow the following steps very carefully.

    - *Collect Email Addresses* – whenever someone calls you about a reservation, whenever they check in to stay overnight, whenever they visit your website you should collect their first name, last name and email address.

    - *Send Emails* – as you continue to build up your list of email addresses you should be sending emails on a routine basis to these people. What do you send them? Well, for starter's you could send them a thank you for their stay/call/visit and then give them a brief survey asking them how their experience was. You can put these people on a monthly newsletter list, send them interesting articles, information about up-coming events at your park, or upcoming events in your area, contests you are holding, special returning visitor discounts, and the list goes on. It costs you nothing to send out these emails other than the time involved in writing up your promotions. Try to get the people to interact with you in some way. (Also, make sure that you do include your company name, physical address, email address, and a way for your customers to unsubscribe so that you are not in violation with email spamming laws – if someone wants to be removed from your list be courteous and do so).

- **The power of email marketing is tremendous and I would recommend starting right now or as soon as you buy the park.** If you are in a destination area and you have a lot of vacancies for an upcoming weekend, then you could send out a quick email to all your prior guests and offer them a discount for those days or announce a special event or ice cream social or whatever. The idea is that within minutes you can get a message out to hundreds if not thousands of people and that may get your phones ringing! In addition, by staying in touch with your prior guests they will remember you and if you are sending them useful and interesting newsletters, tips, or stories they are going to remember you and when they are back in your area you should have a repeat customer.

- Make sure that your emails to these past and potential guests are not just trying to sell them something. Sure you can include a special discount or incentive in your email, but offer them something interesting. It can be a tip on winterizing their RV to washing off the bugs. It can be an interesting event that occurred in your area 50 years ago or is going to occur 10 days from now. It could also be the life story of the guest that stayed their last night. People eat this stuff up!

RV Park Purchase and Sale Agreement

Attached is a sample Purchase and Sale agreement with financing contingencies. Important things for the buyer are the due diligence contingency, financing contingency, survey and legal description, environmental issues, and what is included and not included.

Things to make sure are in contract: have a non compete clause so seller doesn't open an RV Park next door. Have the due diligence period start after you have received all documentation from the seller. Get all existing reports (surveys, phase 1's, title policies, and insurance policies). Have a final accounting so you have all the Profit and Loss statements as of the day of close. Make sure you have enough time and get extension clauses.

When you make an offer and the seller signs, it is a good idea to find out as soon as possible that all of the owner's have signed the contract or that the person that did sign on behalf of company has the authority to do so. I once listed an Mobile Home and RV Park for sale in Kansas. The husband signed the listing agreement. A few weeks later I received a call from the wife explaining that she was half owner and would not agree to sell (they were in divorce proceedings). That was the end of that listing and fortunately I did not have a buyer to also upset with the situation.

Another item you may want to address is who will get the delinquent rents at closing. I often negotiate for these for 25 cents on the dollar depending on the amount and anticipated collection rate.

One possible way to purchase a park is through the use of Lease Options. Basically this will give the owner a way to defer any capitals gains on the sale and still receive a monthly income from the park and have tax shelter through continued depreciation deductions.

This option will not be taxable in most cases until the lease expires or it is executed. In addition if you don't make your payments it will be easier for the owner to get the park back as a foreclosure will not be necessary.

For the purchaser, the lease option may be a way to buy a larger park with less money down and benefit from the appreciation during the lease period which will, in turn, make it easier to finance when the option is exercised. The biggest drawback is the loss of the depreciation deduction but you may deduct the monthly lease payments.

Where to Begin

- Read this book and then reread it again and write down any questions you have.

- Take these questions and go to our new RV Park Investment forum and post them here. We will be answering questions on the forum as well as encouraging other professionals in the industry to do the same as well as other campground owners to give their perspectives.

- Start evaluating as many properties as you have time to – get info from RVParkStore.com and get familiar with looking at income, expenses, and ways to implement the strategies to make properties fit your investment requirements and to make them prosper.

- Visit some parks that are nearby where you live, both poorly run parks as well as those nicer parks and visit with the owners and managers. Learn all you can from them and think about how you could do things differently to operate that park more efficiently and profitably.

- Use as many of the tools and strategies as possible to find parks that will fit your investment criteria.

- Find out what the seller's motivation is in selling as this can be a good indication of potential problems in the park. A bad property for one seller may be your worst nightmare or it may be the perfect turnaround.

- Also when finding out the seller's motivations, this may also help you in structuring the transaction in a way that will benefit both Buyer and Seller.

- When you do put a park under contract, do NOT cut corners in the due diligence process.

Hoping all of your future investments are a SUCCESS!!!

Closing Worksheet *(Great for Future Reference)*

Name of RV Park _____

Physical Address _____

Mailing Address _____

City _____ State _____ Zip _____

Phone _____ Fax _____

Buyer Information:

Buyer's Name _____

Company Name _____

Address _____

City _____ State _____ Zip _____

Phone _____ Fax _____

Email _____ Tax ID# _____

Seller Information:

Seller's Name _____

Company Name _____

New Address _____

City _____ State _____ Zip _____

Phone _____ Fax _____

Email _____ Tax ID# _____

Name _____

Address _____

City _____ State _____ Zip _____

Phone _____ Fax _____

Email _____ Tax ID# _____

Amount of Loan _____ *Date of Loan* _____

Terms _____

Monthly Pmt _____ *Pmt Due Date* _____

Insurance Company Info

Name _____

Address _____

City _____ *State* _____ *Zip* _____

Phone _____ *Fax* _____

Email _____ *Web* _____

Workers Comp Insurance Company Info

Name _____

Address _____

City _____ *State* _____ *Zip* _____

Phone _____ *Fax* _____

Email _____ *Web* _____

Sales Tax Information

Name of Agency _____

Sales Tax Number _____

Name _____

Address _____

City _____ *State* _____ *Zip* _____

Phone _____ *Fax* _____

Email _____ *Web* _____

Business Bank Account

Bank Name _____ Account# _____

Address _____

City _____ State _____ Zip _____

Phone _____ Fax _____

Email _____ Web _____

Credit Card / Merchant Account

Processor Name _____

Merchant ID _____

Phone _____ Fax _____

Email _____ Web _____

List of all Utility Companies, Plumbers, Electricians, Licenses and any other important contacts for the business. Get the account numbers as well as the basic names, addresses, phone numbers.

Filling out this worksheet and keeping it handy and updated will save you time for many years to come.

Sample Business Plan

June 15, 2007

Lender Name & Address

Dear ???,

Thank you for taking the time to look at the financing of the Mobile Home and RV Park we have under contract in City and State. My partner, _____, and I will be forming a new LLC to acquire this property and will make this information available as soon as the new LLC is formed.

I am enclosing the following information for your review.

- Copy of Purchase Agreement

- Copy of Business Plan, Projected Income Statement for 2 years, Management Plan, Management Experience, and Description of Ownership

- Proposed LLC Name: _____

- Copy of my Personal Financial Statement (my partner, will send his PFS to you directly)

- Copy of my Tax Returns for the last 2 years (my partner will send you his)

I will contact you to set up a time to meet with you when I am in town to go over any questions. If you have any additional questions before or after that time please feel free to contact us at your convenience. We look forward to working with you on this loan.

Sincerely,

Company Name & Signature

Business Plan For Company Name

(This is a very basic business plan that I have used successfully for several years)

Presented

December 28, 2006

By: Names of Principals

Address & Contact Info

This business plan contains information that is not to be shared, copied, disclosed or otherwise compromised without the consent of

_____

Chapter I - Executive Summary

Introduction

_____ are purchasing Name of Mobile Home and RV Park in City and State in anticipation of increasing the value of the Property as well as generating an increasing cash flow to provide an excellent return on investment.

Key Considerations

The MH & RV Park is located in the city of _____and state of _____ and is comprised of approximately 100 sites on 28 acres. The existing sites are approximately 40' x 100' and are therefore able to hold any sized Recreational Vehicle or Manufactured Home. Of the 100 homesites, there are currently about 90 occupied sites and 10 sites ready for occupancy. We have based our offering price on the current financial operations and are comfortable that the investment will provide an acceptable cash flow based on current occupancy. We feel through the aggressive management and marketing of the business that we will be able to increase the occupancy significantly which shall, in turn, increase the value of the community as well as the return on investment.

Marketing Objectives

Our marketing objective is to clean the park up, make it an attractive place to live, increase rents to the market level, and fill up any vacant lots in the community. We will do this as follows:

- Cleaning park up & making it an attractive place to live: This will include removing any trash and debris; followed by repairing roads and landscaping as well as adding signage; encouraging residents to clean up, paint, and make their RV's and Homes attractive..

- After the cleanup project is done, we plan to increase the lot rents from the current level of $115 per month to $150-160 per month.

- To fill up the vacant lots we will offer incentives to prospective residents to bring their home into the community through free or reduced site rent, moving allowances, and other special promotions. In addition we may purchase good used repossessed homes from lenders and/or dealers and move them into the community. These homes will then be refurbished and be offered to potential residents for sale, lease, or lease-to-own.

Expected Accomplishments

We anticipate that it will take approximately 1 year to get the park stabilized and running smoothly. Upon reaching this level we expect to receive a 40% plus return on our investment as well as increase the value of the community to over $1,000,000.

Required Capital

Initial Purchase of Community: $750,000 purchase price. The purchasers of the community will contribute a total of $150,000 and will seek financing for the balance of the purchase price in the amount of $600,000. In addition, the purchaser's expect to spend in the range of $50,000 to $100,000 in making improvements and stabilizing the project. This amount will be self-funded initially.

Chapter II - The Business

Problem Statement

The largest hurdle or problem that we anticipate is finding quality residents that pay their rent and/or home payment on time. Our competition is other mobile home and recreational vehicle parks in the area as well as other means of residential housing. Our solution to this is to make this an attractive community as well as make it affordable compared to other housing solutions. We will do this by keeping our rates and prices near that of the competition as well as offering creative solutions to those that demonstrate a good worth ethic as well as a desire to be financially responsible.

Qualifications of the owners

Insert a brief resume of you background, education, and accomplishments.

Management & Operations

1. *Co-Managers: Name of Principals:* The Co-Managers will be responsible for overseeing the onsite manager and the purchase of homes, overseeing the repair and delivery of the homes, and the sales of the homes. The will also be responsible for the overall profitability of the Mobile Home and RV Park and any financing transactions.

2. *Onsite Managers: To Be Determined:* The onsite manager shall be responsible for record keeping, collecting and depositing rent, property maintenance, showing available lots and homes to prospective residents, enforcing rules and regulations of the community, handling resident problems and questions, and all duties involved with managing the property.

Objectives

The overall objective is to maximize the profitability of this community to provide an excellent return on investment as well as increase the value of the community for a possible sale in the future.

Legal Form

Name of Principals will form a new LLC with a proposed name of _____. It is anticipated that we will each own an equal percentage of the LLC.

Chapter III - Finances

Assumptions

The following assumptions were made in preparing these forecasts:

- 2006 Space Rental Income: Based on 90 occupied lots @ $140 per month.

- 2007 Space Rental Income: Based on 93 occupied lots @ $160 per month.

- Expenses: Based on prior owners' projections and our experience.

Profit & Loss Projections

	Current	End Of 2006	End Of 2007
Income			
Mh Space Rent	$111,585	$151,200	$178,560
Total Income	**$111,585**	**$151,200**	**$178,560**
Expenses			
Advertising	$0	$1,200	1,260
Insurance	$2,837	3,000	3,150
Legal & Professional	$0	2,400	2,520
Maintenance & Repairs	$14,924	12,000	12,600
Office Expenses	$514	600	630
Payroll Expenses	$0	15,000	15,750
Property Taxes	$2,817	4,000	4,200
Telephone	$368	700	735
Travel Expenses	$0	3,000	3,150
Utilities	$12,098	12,703	13,338
Total Expenses	**$33,558**	**$54,603**	**$57,333**
Net Operating Income	$78,027	$96,597	$121,227
1st Mortgage(600k, 25 Yr, 7.00%)	$28,236	$28,236	$28,236
Net Cash Flow	$49,791	$68,361	$92,991
Cash Invested	$150,000	$200,000	$200,000
Return On Investment	33.19%	34.18%	46.50%

Sample Purchase and Sale Agreement

For valuable consideration, the receipt and adequacy of which is hereby acknowledged, this Agreement dated _____ is hereby made by and between NAME OF PURCHASER, and/or their assigns or nominee, (hereinafter "PURCHASER") and NAME OF SELLER (hereinafter "SELLER").

WITNESSETH:

WHEREAS, SELLER owns an RV Park and improvements situated thereon, in CITY AND STATE.

WHEREAS, SELLER desires to sell, transfer and assign to PURCHASER the land, together with all improvements thereon (hereinafter referred to as the "Real Estate") and personal property (hereinafter referred to as "Personal Property"), and;

WHEREAS, PURCHASER desires to acquire from SELLER said Real Estate and Personal Property.

NOW THEREFORE, in consideration of the mutual promises herein contained, the parties hereto agree as follows:

1. ***Sale Of Real Estate And Personal Property.*** Subject to the terms and conditions of this Agreement, SELLER hereby agrees to sell, convey, transfer, assign and deliver to PURCHASER, and PURCHASER agrees to purchase from SELLER, the Real Estate and Personal Property, as defined below:

    Real Estate defined: The land, including all improvements, legally described and identified on Schedule A (attached hereto and made a part hereof). Notwithstanding the foregoing, the definition of the Real Estate hereunder shall not include any Hazardous Substance, as defined in paragraph 13(g) of this Agreement, and under no circumstances shall PURCHAS-

ER be deemed to have consented or agreed to take title to or ownership on any Real Estate, or portion thereof, which is found to be contaminated with or by any Hazardous Substance;

Personal Property defined: The non-real estate assets described and identified on Schedule B (attached hereto and made a part hereof) are the Personal Property subject to this Agreement. Notwithstanding the foregoing, the definition of the Personal Property hereunder shall not include any Hazardous Substance, as defined in paragraph 13(g) of this Agreement, and under no circumstances shall PURCHASER be deemed to have consented or agreed to take title to or ownership on any Personal Property, or portion thereof, which is found to be contaminated with or by any Hazardous Substance;

2. ***Purchase Price:*** The total purchase price for the Real Estate and Personal Property shall be PURCHASE PRICE ($), plus and/or minus the Prorations, as such term is hereinafter defined (the "Purchase Price"), which shall be paid as follows:

    a) The sum of $5,000.00 shall be paid by check from PURCHASER within Five (5) days of the date of this Agreement, which amount shall serve as an Earnest money deposit, subject to the provisions of paragraph 3(c) below, and applied to the balance of the purchase price due at closing. Said Earnest money deposit shall be held in escrow by national title company, as escrow agent, that is reasonably acceptable to PURCHASER and SELLER.

    b) At closing, the PURCHASER shall pay to SELLER, by wire, cashier's or certified check, the balance of the Purchase Price with a wire transfer, cashier's check, certified check or other good funds in the amount of PURCHASE PRICE LESS EARNEST MONEY DEPOSIT ($). Purchase Price to reflect (a) credits to PURCHASER for any liabilities or charges assumed, and (b) credits to SELLER for any amounts prepaid or otherwise credited for the benefit of PURCHASER; provided, however, that the Prorations shall not include any adjustments for the benefit of SELLER for any unpaid rents or assessments. The amount of any general real estate taxes not then ascertainable, if any, shall be adjusted on the basis of 105% of the most recent ascertainable general real estate taxes.

c) The "Prorations shall be defined to mean prepaid rents, prepaid assessments, security deposits, prepaid or unpaid water and other utility or fuel charges, prepaid or unpaid service contracts, general or special real estate taxes or assessments, and other unpaid taxes. The Prorations shall be adjustments to the Purchase Price to reflect (a) credits to PURCHASER for any liabilities or charges assumed, and (c) credits to SELLER for mounts prepaid or otherwise credited for the benefit of PURCHASER; provided, however, that the Prorations shall not include any adjustments for the benefit of SELLER for any unpaid rents or assessments. The amount of any general real estates taxes not then ascertainable, if any, shall be adjusted on the basis of 105% of the most recent ascertainable general real estate taxes.

3. ***Purchaser's Rights Of Inspection, Loan Approval, And Cancellation.*** *(if the sale involves seller financing insert the terms and conditions here)*

a) PURCHASER may inspect or cause to be inspected the condition of the Real Estate and all improvements and Personal Property;

b) PURCHASER may inspect or cause to be inspected all other documents and materials relating to the Real Estate and Personal Property, with SELLER to deliver any such documents or materials to PURCHASER within seven (7) days of PURCHASER'S request;

c) PURCHASER may cancel this Agreement for any reason, at the sole discretion of PURCHASER, within Sixty (60) days of acceptance of this Agreement by SELLER. After the initial Sixty (60) day inspection period, PURCHASER may cancel this Agreement during the next Thirty (30) day period in the event that PURCHASER does not obtain a loan approval for the purchase of the Real Estate and Personal Property that is satisfactory to PURCHASER, and the determination of an acceptable loan shall be in the PURCHASER'S sole discretion. In the event that PURCHASER elects to cancel this Agreement during the initial 60 day inspection period, or during the additional 30 days designated for loan approval, this paragraph shall serve as authority to the escrow agent from the SELLER to act upon the "single order" of PURCHASER to distribute the Earnest money to PURCHASER. Additionally, this paragraph shall serve as the SELLER'S release of the escrow agent from liability for disbursing the Earnest money to PURCHASER.

SELLER shall allow PURCHASER, or PURCHASER'S representatives, access or provide documents for review, whichever the case may be, to the Real Estate and Personal Property, at all reasonable times and cooperate with PURCHASER'S efforts to conduct the inspections permitted herein.

4. **Title Insurance, Survey, And Environmental Study.**

   a) **Title Insurance:** Within Thirty (30) days from the date of this Agreement, SELLER shall deliver a commitment for an ALTA owner's policy of title insurance that is reasonably acceptable to PURCHASER (together with legible copies of all easements and restrictions of record identified by the commitment), in the full amount of the purchase price, evidencing SELLER'S good and merchantable title to the Real Estate. In the event that this proposed transaction does close, at closing, SELLER shall be responsible for the cost of title insurance.

   b) **Survey:** Within Thirty (30) days from the date of this Agreement, SELLER shall deliver to PURCHASER an ALTA Survey of the Real Estate. SELLER shall be responsible for the cost of survey.

   c) **Environmental study:** PURCHASER may obtain, at PURCHASER'S expense, an environmental study of the Real Estate. PURCHASER shall be responsible for the cost of the environmental study.

5. **The Closing:** Subject to PURCHASER'S right to terminate this Agreement, as set forth in Paragraph 3(c) above, the closing of this transaction shall be held no later than 30 days after the PURCHASER'S right of inspection and cancellation period expires, as described in Paragraph 3, above, unless earlier extended in writing and signed by mutual agreement of the SELLER and the PURCHASER. The closing shall take

place at the title company serving as escrow agent for the earnest deposit. The time of the closing shall be a mutually convenient time for the PURCHASER and SELLER.

6. ***Purchaser's Closing Instruments:*** At closing, PURCHASER shall deliver to SELLER the following instruments:

    a) A certified, cashier's check, or wire transfer for the amount required by Paragraph 2(b).

    b) Any other instruments reasonably necessary to complete the transaction contemplated hereby.

7. ***Seller's Closing Instruments:*** At the closing, SELLER shall deliver to PURCHASER the following documents:

    a) A Warranty Deed reasonably acceptable to PURCHASER conveying good title in the Real Estate as described in Schedule A, and a transfer of title agreement reasonably acceptable to PURCHASER conveying good title in the Personal Property as described in Schedule B;

    b) Any other instruments reasonably necessary to complete the transaction contemplated hereby.

8. ***Possession:*** PURCHASER shall take possession of all of the Real Estate and Personal Property at closing.

9. ***Prorations, Transfer Taxes, And Closing Costs:*** Prorations shall take place at the time of closing. All deposits shall be transferred to PURCHASER at closing, including but not limited to security deposits from residents and advanced rental deposits from residents. PURCHASER and SELLER shall pay their usual and customary portion of transfer taxes at the time of closing. All remaining closing costs which

have not been addressed by this Agreement shall be shared equally by PURCHASER and SELLER.

10. ***Cross Indemnification:***   SELLER hereby agrees to indemnify PURCHASER and hold and save PURCHASER harmless from and against all liabilities, debts, claims, actions, causes or action, losses, damages, and attorney's fees, now existing or that may hereafter arise from or grow out of SELLER'S past ownership of the Real Estate and Personal Property, that are of the subject of this Agreement, and which occurred through the date of closing. PURCHASER hereby agrees to indemnify SELLER and hold and save SELLER harmless from and against all liabilities, debts, claims, actions, or causes of action, losses, damages, and attorney's fees, that may arise from or grow out of PURCHASER'S ownership of the Real Estate and Personal Property, that are the subject of this Agreement after the date of closing.

SELLER and PURCHASER acknowledge that this contemplated transaction includes only the sale and purchase of the Real Estate and Personal Property, and the parties don not intend that PURCHASER be deemed a successor of SELLER with respect to any liabilities of SELLER to any third parties. Accordingly, PURCHASER shall, neither assume nor be liable for, any payments and benefits to past and/or present employees of SELLER in connection with the Business being conducted on or from the Property as may have accrued through the Closing Date, including, but not limited to, salaries, wages, commission, bonuses, vacation pay, health and welfare contributions, pensions, profit sharing, severance or termination pay, taxes or any other form of compensation or fringe benefit.

11. ***Commissions Due.****(If there is a brokerage company involved then this needs to be changed).* PURCHASER represents and warrants to SELLER, and SELLER represents and warrants to PURCHASER, that no commission is due as a result of this transaction contemplated hereby and no real estate brokerage company has been used by either PURCHASER or SELLER to facilitate this transaction. PURCHASER and SELLER shall indemnify and hold each other harmless, from all claims or damages for any brokerage commissions and/or fees being claimed, and arising out of this transaction resulting from the actions of the defaulting party.

12. ***Purchaser's Representations And Warranties:*** PURCHASER hereby represents and warrants to SELLER as follows:

    a)   PURCHASER warrants that it is a limited liability company duly organized, validly existing, and in good standing under the laws of the State of _____;

    b)   PURCHASER warrants that it has full power and authority to execute, deliver and perform this Agreement;

    c)   PURCHASER warrants that the execution, delivery and performance of this Agreement by PURCHASER has been duly authorized by all requisite actions on the part of PURCHASER;

    d)   PURCHASER warrants that it has no judgment against it in any court of law or equity, nor does PURCHASER have knowledge of any claims that may lead to the institution of legal proceedings against it;

    e)   PURCHASER warrants that all representations and warranties of PURCHASER in this Agreement are true, accurate and complete in all material respects as of the date hereof, and will be true, accurate and complete in all material respects as of the date of closing.

All representations and warranties of PURCHASER contained in this Agreement, and all remedial provisions contained herein, shall be deemed remade at closing and shall survive the closing.

13. *Seller's Representations And Warranties:*   SELLER hereby represents and warrants to PURCHASER as follows:

a)   SELLER warrants that, so long as this Agreement is in effect, SELLER will not negotiate or contract with any other person or entity for the sale and purchase of the Real Estate and Personal Property;

b)   SELLER warrants that to the best of SELLER'S knowledge there are no claims, actions, suits or proceedings pending or threatened on account of or as a result of SELLER'S ownership of the Real Estate and Personal Property, which, if adversely determined, would have an adverse impact on the value of the Real Estate and Personal Property, or would prevent or hinder the consummation of the transaction contemplated herein;

c)   SELLER warrants that to the best of SELLER'S knowledge the records of the Real Estate and Personal Property constitute a true and accurate representation of the financial condition of the manufactured home community as of the date of said statements and records;

d)   SELLER warrants that to the best of SELLER'S knowledge SELLER has good and merchantable title in fee simple to the Real Estate and Personal Property, that are subject to this Agreement, and the SELLER has not entered into any leases, licenses, easements or other agreements, recorded or unrecorded, granting rights to any parties in any of the assets, other than to renters in the manufactured housing community, and no person or other entity has any right to possession or occupancy of any of the assets, other than renters in the community;

e) SELLER warrants that to the best of SELLER'S knowledge there exists no violation of any Federal, State, County, or any other laws, or ordinances, with respect to the use and operation of the Real Estate and Personal Property as a manufactured housing community;

f) SELLER warrants that to the best of SELLER'S knowledge SELLER is not in default under or in violation of any contract, commitment, or restriction to which they are a party or by which they are bound, which default or violation would have a material and adverse effect on this transaction;

g) SELLER warrants that to the best of SELLER'S knowledge there has never been and there are currently no hazardous substances, generated, stored, buried, placed, held, located or disposed of on, under or at the Real Estate and the Real Estate has never been used as a dump site, and there are no, nor have there ever been any, underground storage tanks in or on the Real Estate.

The definition of "Hazardous substances" shall mean all hazardous or toxic materials, substances, pollutants, contaminants, or wastes currently identified as a hazardous substance or waste in the Comprehensive Environmental Response, Compensation and Liability Act of 1980 (commonly known as "CERCA"), as amended, the Superfund Amendments and Preauthorization Act (commonly known as "SARA"), as amended, the Resource Conservation and Recovery Act (commonly known as "RARA"), as amended, or any other federal, state or local legislation or ordinances applicable to the Real Estate or Personal Property;

h) SELLER warrants that to the best of SELLER'S knowledge the Real Estate has at least _____ Recreational Vehicle Sites and has zoning and all regulatory approvals for at least _____ Recreational Vehicle Sites and there are no pending requirements that must be satisfied in order to maintain such approval. Additionally, SELLER warrants that there are no regulatory or non-regulatory restrictions that would limit the PURCHASER'S ability to replace a Recreational Vehile if one or more of the _____ sites becomes vacant. Additionally, SELLER warrants that to the best of SELLER'S knowledge all power supplies/systems owned by SELLER meet the current code requirements as well as any change mandates that are in effect. Additionally, SELLER warrants that to the best of SELLER'S knowledge there are no existing or pending regulatory requirements that must be satisfied for SELLER to complete this Agreement with PURCHASER. Additionally, SELLER warrants that to the best of SELLER'S knowledge there is no other study, report or finding which indicates that any portion of the Real Estate is located in a floodplain or is unsuitable for building purposes;

    i)   SELLER warrants that to the best of SELLER'S knowledge the water and sewer systems, together with all mechanical systems serving the subject Real Estate and Personal Property, are in sound operating condition, free from hidden or latent defects, and are adequate in size and performance to properly serve the needs of the existing manufactured home community; and

    j)   SELLER warrants that to the best of SELLER'S knowledge all representations and warranties of SELLER in this Agreement are true, accurate and complete in all material respects as of the date hereof, and will be true, accurate and complete in all material respects as of the date of closing.

All representations and warranties of SELLER contained in this Agreement, and all remedial provisions contained herein, shall be deemed remade at closing and shall survive the closing.

14. ***Addiitional Provisions:***   In this section you will want to include such things as:

- Seller Training – Time/Costs

- Observation Periods

Anything else that may be property specific or out of the norm.

15. ***General Terms:***   The following general provisions shall also apply to this Agreement:

    a)   All notices that may be required by this Agreement shall be sent to the respective parties at the addresses appearing below:

    "PURCHASER"   "SELLER "

Purchaser Info   Seller Info

Any such notices shall be (i) personally delivered to the office set forth above, in which case they shall be deemed delivered on the date of delivery to said offices, (ii) sent by certified mail, return receipt requested, in which case they shall be deemed delivered three (3) days after deposit in the U.S. mail, postage prepaid, (iii) sent by facsimile, in which case they shall be deemed delivered on the date of transmission (if before 5:00 p.m. CST) or (iv) sent by air courier (Federal Express or like service), in which case they shall be deemed delivered on the date of actual delivery. Either party may change the address to which any such notice is to be delivered by furnishing written notice of such change to the other party via one of the above methods in compliance with the foregoing provisions;

b) In the event that a dispute arises over the terms of this Agreement, the parties agree to submit to binding arbitration to resolve such dispute. The arbitration shall be conducted in accordance with the Expedited Procedures of the Commercial Arbitration Rules of the American Arbitration Association at a hearing to be held in or near Phoenix, Arizona and the laws of Arizona shall govern. Any decision reached from such arbitration shall have the same binding authority as if it were decided by a court of competent jurisdiction. The non-prevailing party shall pay all costs, including reasonable attorney's fees, of the prevailing party;

c) In the event the transaction contemplated hereby does not close or is terminated due to a default by SELLER,

PURCHASER shall be entitled to immediate return of the Earnest Money and may pursue all its rights and remedies at law and in equity, including, without limitation, specific performance. In the event the transaction contemplated hereby does not close or is terminated due to a default by PURCHASER in the performance of its obligations under the Agreement, SELLER, as their sole remedy, either at law or in equity, shall be entitled to retain the Earnest Money as liquidated damages. In the event of a default by either party hereto, the party not in default shall give notice thereof to the defaulting party and an opportunity to cure for a period of five (5) days following the delivery of notice, prior to exercising any right or remedy to which the party not in default may be entitled;

d) PURCHASER may nominate and/or assign its rights under this Agreement.

e) Either PURCHASER or SELLER may record this Agreement in the county where the Real Estate is located, provided that the party choosing to record pays all county recording fees associated with the recording.

f) This Agreement constitutes the entire agreement between the parties pertaining to the subject matter contained herein and supersedes all prior and contemporaneous agreements or representations whether written or oral;

g) This Agreement may only be modified if the modification is made in writing and signed by both PUR-

CHASER and SELLER. No oral modifications shall be permitted;

h) This Agreement is binding upon, and inures to the benefit of the parties hereto and their heirs, executors, administrators, successors, and assigns;

i) Each party, by its execution of this Agreement, represents that by signing this Agreement, they are acting on the PURCHASER'S or SELLER'S behalf, whichever shall apply, and they are duly authorized and empowered by any necessary acts to make this Agreement binding;

j) For purposes of this Agreement, the term "Day" shall mean calendar day, unless otherwise specified. The time in which any act provided by this Agreement is to be done shall be computed by excluding the first day and including the last, unless the last day is a Saturday, Sunday, or Holiday, in which case it also shall be excluded. If any deadline set forth herein falls on a Saturday, Sunday, or Holiday, the deadline shall be extended to the next business day;

k) This Agreement is intended to be performed in accordance with, and only to the extent permitted by all applicable laws, ordinances, rules and circumstances. If for any reason and to any extent any portion of this Agreement shall be held to be invalid or unenforceable, the remainder of this Agreement shall be enforced as if such invalid or unenforceable provision did not exist, and such valid and enforceable remainder shall be enforced to the greatest extent as permitted by law;

l)   Time is of the essence of this Agreement, and of each provision thereof;

m)   This Agreement may be executed in one or more counterparts;

n)   This offer shall expire and become null and void if not accepted by SELLER and delivered to PURCHASER within seven (7) days of the date of this Agreement;

IN WITNESS WHEREOF, the parties hereto have executed this Agreement, and agree to its terms.

PURCHASER   SELLER

_____   _____   _____   _____

Signature   Date: Signature   Date:

PURCHASER   SELLER

_____   _____   _____   _____

Signature   Date: Signature   Date:

Schedule A: Real Property Descriptions:

Address:

Approximately _____ Acres

Legal Description:

Schedule B: Personal Property Description:

www.ingramcontent.com/pod-product-compliance
Lightning Source LLC
Chambersburg PA
CBHW021102210326
41598CB00016B/1290